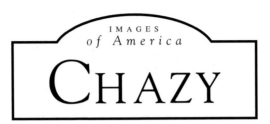

IMAGES
of America

CHAZY

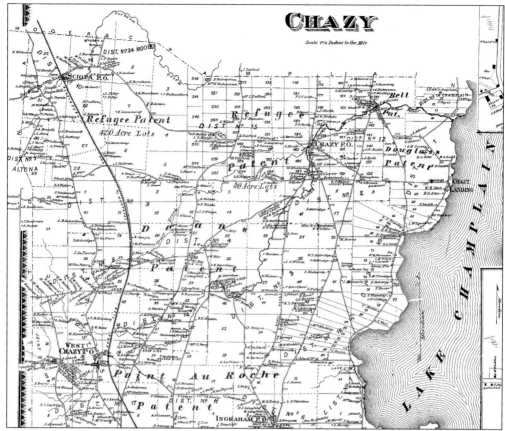

The maps of Chazy, Sciota, and West Chazy are from *Atlas of Clinton County New York*, published by F.W. Beers, A.D. Ellis, and G.G. Soule in 1869.

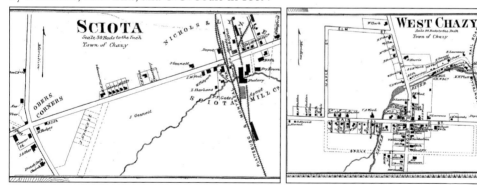

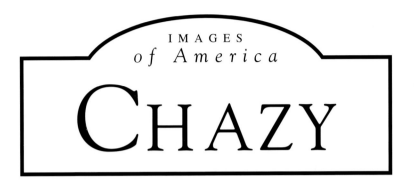

IMAGES
of America

CHAZY

Christina M. Trombly

ARCADIA
PUBLISHING

Published by Arcadia Publishing
Charleston, South Carolina

Printed in the United States of America

Library of Congress Catalog Card Number: 2003111118

For all general information, contact Arcadia Publishing:
Telephone 843-853-2070
Fax 843-853-0044
E-mail sales@arcadiapublishing.com
For customer service and orders:
Toll-Free 1-888-313-2665

Visit us on the Internet at www.arcadiapublishing.com

On the cover: Pictured on the front cover are, from left to right, the following:
Rev. Peter J. H. Meyers, Elizabeth B. McCarger (teacher 1905–1906), and Laura Graves.
On the back cover are, from left to right, Adaline Trombly (wife of Harrison Fitch) and
Matilda Wilson (wife of Edgar Graves).

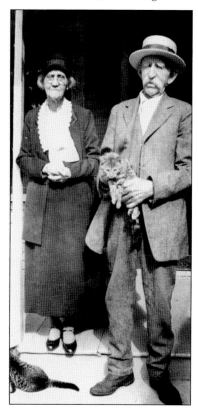

Shown are Della and Simeon Trombly.

CONTENTS

ACKNOWLEDGMENTS

I want to thank the members of the Bicentennial Publication Committee, who helped me with all parts of this book: Helen Saxe Booth, Robert Booth, Bob Cheeseman, Marie Laramic Gennett, Jane Fulton Hess, Ralph "Pete" Hubbell, Nancy LaPier LeClair, David K. Martin, Tim Neverett, John Patterson, and William "Skip" Saxe.

Chazy Central Rural School English teacher Kathryn D. Burnam and her sophomore class submitted essays after speaking with senior citizens in our community. Thanks go to Alice Lou Sanger, Helen Saxe Booth, Pete Hubbell, and my daughters, Tiffany and Tara Trombly, for help during the final process. I appreciate the computer help of Charles Dumar. Carolyn Harding, of the Plattsburgh Chamber of Commerce, provided valuable information on the area. Joseph Lavorando was kind enough to review consent forms for the town. Many thanks go to the people of Chazy and beyond who have shared their stories and pictures. Thanks go to my family for continued support and love. A special thank-you goes to Marie Gennett for all her help while I learned the job of historian. She was the inspiration for this book; her stories of growing up are so wonderful and funny that I needed to share them. A *History of the Town of Chazy*, by Nell Jane Barnett Sullivan and David Kendall Martin, was published 30 years ago and gives the reader a full understanding of our area and its place in history.

—Christina M. Trombly

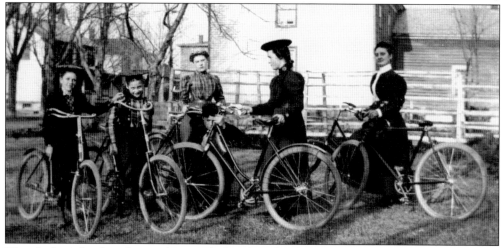

Warmly dressed girls gather outdoors with their bicycles. (Image, David Martin.)

INTRODUCTION

This is a book of memories of the people of Chazy. In March 1804, the New York State legislature chartered a town in the northeast corner of the state and called it Chazy. The town included the hamlets of West Chazy, Sciota, Chazy Landing, Ingraham, and Suckortown. Bordered on the east by Lake Champlain and on the north by Canada, the area was discovered by Europeans in the 1600s. The town takes its name from a French soldier, Captain de Chazy, who was killed near the mouth of a river that also bears his name.

With the bicentennial year approaching, I wanted to do something for the town to mark this special occasion. The job of historian is very rewarding, and I discovered many wonderful pictures and bits of history that I was not aware existed. People were sharing their stories with me, and I felt privileged. I needed other people to hear these stories and see images of our town as it once was. I asked for help and received more than I ever expected. Thanks to the Internet, I started receiving messages from people who no longer live here but still have fond memories and from those who have always lived here. Many people felt their stories were not important enough to share. They were not rich or famous. They lived simple lives. Their stories, however, are rich, and in sharing them with you, I have endeavored to make those people famous.

I asked the sophomore English class at Chazy Central Rural School to consider interviewing senior citizens in our community and to write an essay on that interview. Several students tackled the assignment, and their contributions have been included. It is a hope of mine to get younger people interested in their past. Many people come here researching their genealogy and wish they had taken the time to talk to relatives who are no longer with us. We need to pay attention to the people we care about and learn their stories. History is recorded, but the stories are not. The committee made an effort to use material submitted, but because of space limitations, some may have been omitted. All materials donated to this office will be saved for future generations.

Finally, I would like to mention the importance of recording information on photographs. Many of the images in this collection were unlabeled, and we have no way of identifying these special people and places. Therefore, take the time to identify your photographs with archival pens so the images will preserve a place in time that is special to you. I hope Chazy makes you laugh, cry, and say wow, and inspires you to ask questions. I dedicate this book to all the people of Chazy, past, present, and future.

—Christina M. Trombly

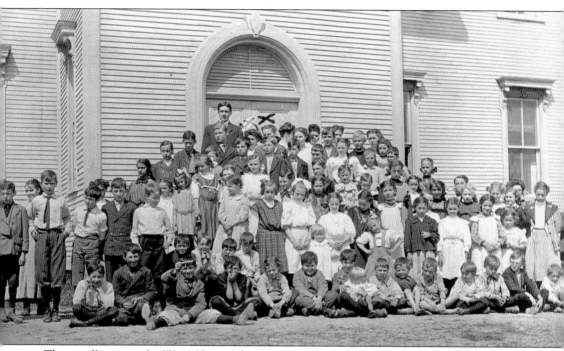

The enrollment at the West Chazy School was sizable c. 1900.

One

1804–1899

"Chazy, a Post-Township of Clinton County, 186 miles N. of Albany . . . was erected in 1804, from part of Champlain, and its boundaries were altered in 1808. The whole population of this Town in 1810 was 1466. . . . The soil is pretty good, and the inhabitants are hardy, industrious farmers, who make the most of their clothing in the household way."—From the 1813 *Gazetteer of New York*, pages 158–159.

"Chazy, a Post-Township of Clinton County, 12 miles N. of Plattsburgh [contains] 30 or 40 houses, 4 stores, the Post Office, 2 churches, (1 of stone and 1 of wood) a school-house, and 2 mills. Population 2,318; 11 school districts, and 651 children between 5 and 15 years of age; 1668 cattle, 257 horses, 3169 sheep: 10,089 yards of cloth made in families: 3 grist mills, 6 saw mills, 2 fulling mills, 3 carding machines, and 34 asheries."—From the 1824 *Gazetteer of the State of New York*, page 106.

"Chazy, West Chazy, and Chazy Landing are villages; the first two have post offices. Chazy Landing, lies on the lake . . . and has a dock and storehouse, a dry good and grocery store, and 15 to 20 dwellings. West Chazy, late Lawrence's Mills . . . contains 1 Methodist church, 1 store, 1 temperance house, 1 grist mill, 2 saw mills, 1 trip hammer, carding and cloth dressing mill, and 30 dwellings."—From the 1836 *Gazetteer of the State of New York*, page 398.

"Chazy . . . contains about 250 inhabitants, 50 dwelling houses, 1 Congregational and 1 Methodist church, 2 taverns, 3 stores, 2 grist mills, 1 trip hammer works and 2 tanneries. Blue Limestone or Marble, is found in abundance . . . equal in beauty to Irish Marble. West Chazy [contains] 1 Presbyterian church, 1 tavern, 7 stores, 1 woolen factory, 1 grist mill, 1 saw mill, and 30 to 40 dwellings."—From the 1842 *Gazetteer of the State of New York*, pages 115 and 419.

"Chazy . . . Altona was taken off in 1857. Potsdam sandstone underlies the w. part. . . . Sciota, is a station in the N.W. corner of the town. . . . Station on the Plattsburgh and Montreal branch of Vt. Central, and Vt. & Can. R.R."—From the 1872 *Gazetteer of the State of New York*, page 230.

An Act for dividing the Town of Champlain
in the County of Clinton.

Be it enacted by the people of the State of New York
represented in Senate and Assembly that from and after
the first Monday of April next All that part of the Town of
Champlain in the County of Clinton on the South side of a line
beginning on the Lake shore at the southeast boundary of
Lot Number fifteen said Lot being a part of the Lands grant
ed by the State of New York to certain Canadian and Nova-
scotia refugees thence by the south line of said Lot Westerly and on the North line of a Tract of land known by
Bells Patent originally granted to Hezekiah Tuttle and
Westerly upon the North line of Eighty Acre Lots, to wit,
Numbers One hundred and forty five, One hundred and
sixty three, One hundred and seventy eight, one hundred
and forty three, One hundred and ninety five, Two hundred and seventeen and Two hundred and thirty two and
from the Northwest corner of the last mentioned Lot a straight
line to the northeast corner of Lot Number Eight a four
hundred and twenty acre Lot a part of those Lands grant
ed as aforesaid from thence Westerly on the north line of Lots
Number Eight, twenty five, thirty two, forty nine, sixty three,
Eighty, Eighty seven, One hundred and four, One hundred
and twelve, One hundred and twenty nine, One hundred
and thirty eight, One hundred and fifty five, one hundred
and sixty six, One hundred and eighty three and One hundred and ninety two and from thence on the same course
to the west line of said Town shall be and is hereby erected
into a seperate Town by the name of Chazy and that the
first Town meeting shall be held at the house of Eleazer
Graves in said Town.

And be it further enacted that that part of
the said Town of Champlain situated north of the line
before described and West of the following line to wit
Beginning at the Northwest corner of Lot Number Eight

The handwritten charter of the town of Chazy is entitled "An Act for Dividing the
Town of Champlain in the County of Clinton." It is dated March 1804. The inset

10

before described and running northerly upon the west line of Lots Number nine, ten eleven twelve, thirteen fourteen fifteen and sixteen to the Province of Canada shall be and is hereby erected into a seperate Town by the name of Mooers and that the first Town meeting shall be held at the house of Shaden in said Town And that all the remainder of the Town of Champlain shall be and remain a seperate Town by the name of Champlain and that the next town meeting be held at the house of Samuel Hicks in the said Town.

And be it further enacted that as soon as may be after the first Tuesday in April next the Supervisors and Overseers of the poor of the aforesaid Towns on notice being previously given by the said Supervisors for that purpose shall meet and divide the poor and money belonging to the said Town of Champlain previous to the division thereof agreeable to the last tax list and that each of the said Towns shall forever thereafter respectively support their own poor.

And be it further enacted that the lines of the said Towns of Champlain and Chazy do and shall extend East to the East boundary of the State of New York. —

State of New York
In Senate March 16th 1804
This Bill having been read the third time
Resolved that the Bill do pass
By order of the Senate—

Jer V Rensselaer President

State of New York
In Assembly March 9th 1804
This Bill having been read the third time
Resolved, That the Bill do pass
By orders of the Assembly.

Alexr Sheldon Speaker

(above, lower left) shows the signature of Gov. George Clinton.

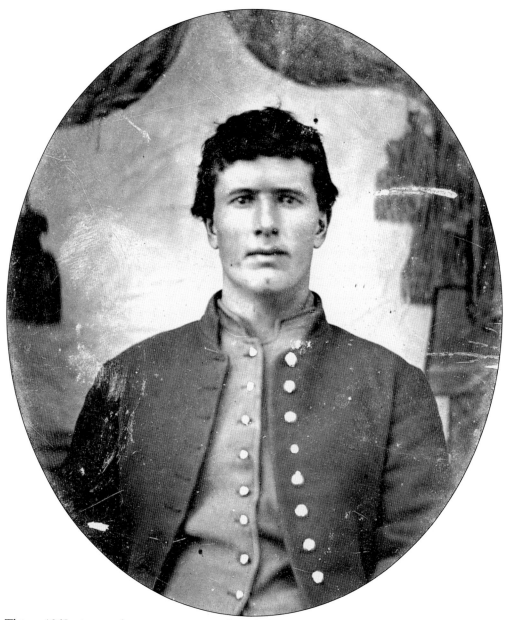

This *c.* 1860s tintype shows a young man identified simply as a Civil War hero.

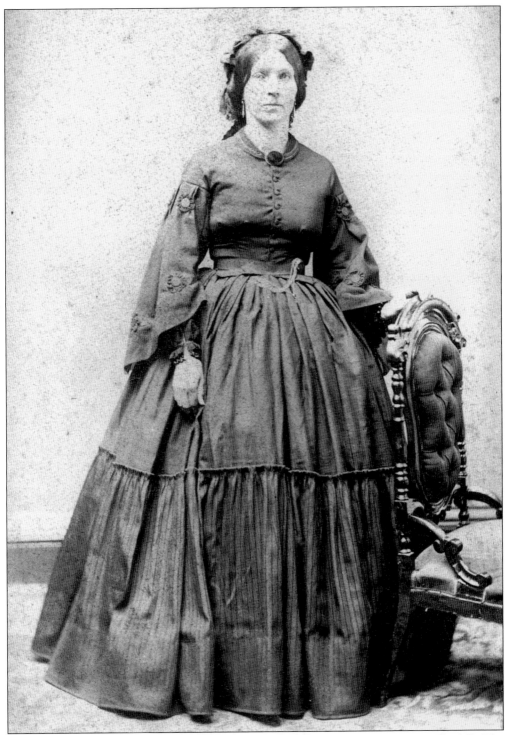

The partially visible name written below this *c.* 1860 portrait is perhaps E.V. Blasdell. The woman's serious face is framed by fine hair. Note her long fingers and her elegant dress, brooch, and earrings. A chair was often included in formal portraits.

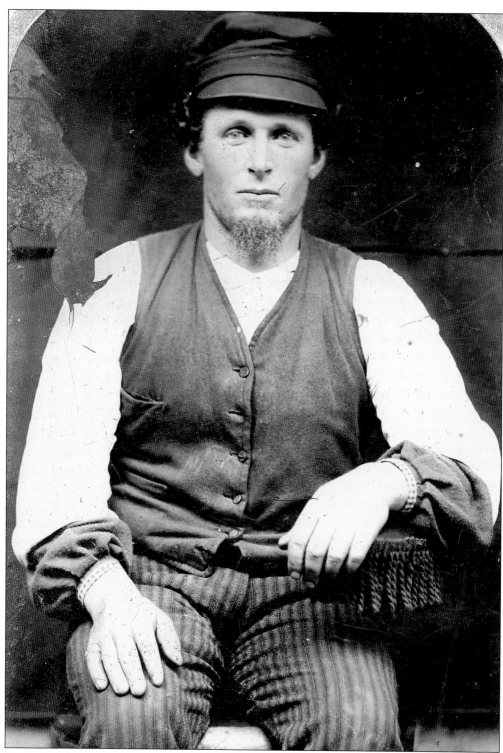

Sitting for his portrait is a man with a light goatee and dark curly hair, mostly covered by his cap. Note his strong hands, striped trousers, and pocketed vest. This tintype dates from *c.* 1860.

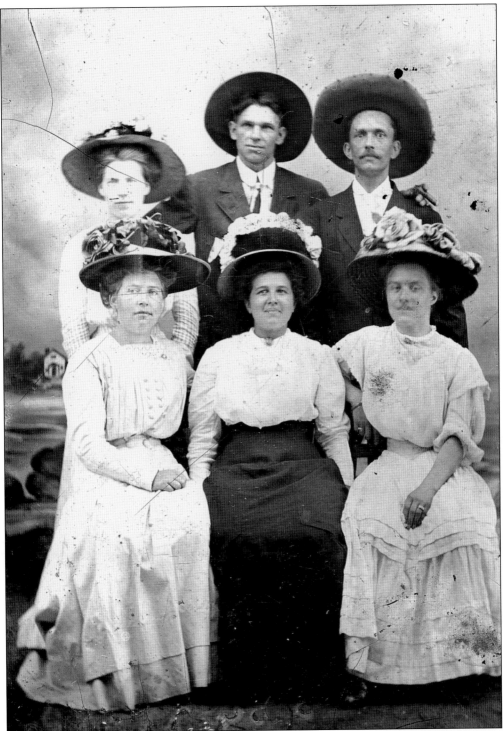

Dressed in their finest clothes, four women and two men pose for what might be a family portrait. Note the variety of hats on the women and the wide-brimmed ones on the men. This tintype was made sometime between the 1860s and the 1880s.

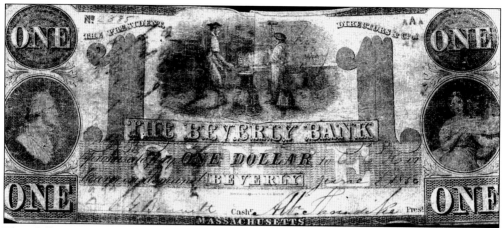

This dollar, issued by the Beverly (Massachusetts) Bank, appears to be dated June of either 1850 or 1856.

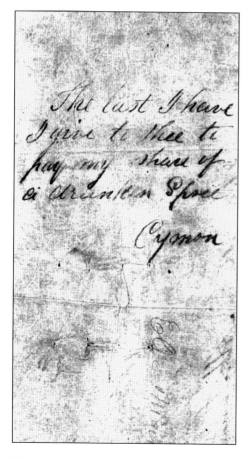

The back of the bill contains the following handwritten message: "The last I have I give to thee to pay my share of a drunkin spree." The note is signed "Cymon."

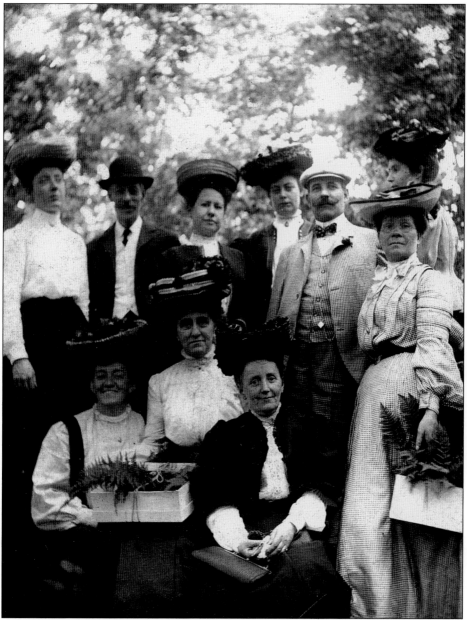

Three or more of these people are smiling, which is unusual in early photographs. Two of the women in the foreground are holding a box of ferns. The men sport mustaches and wear suits with ties and vests. Equally well dressed, the women wear their best hats. (Image, Matt Clark.)

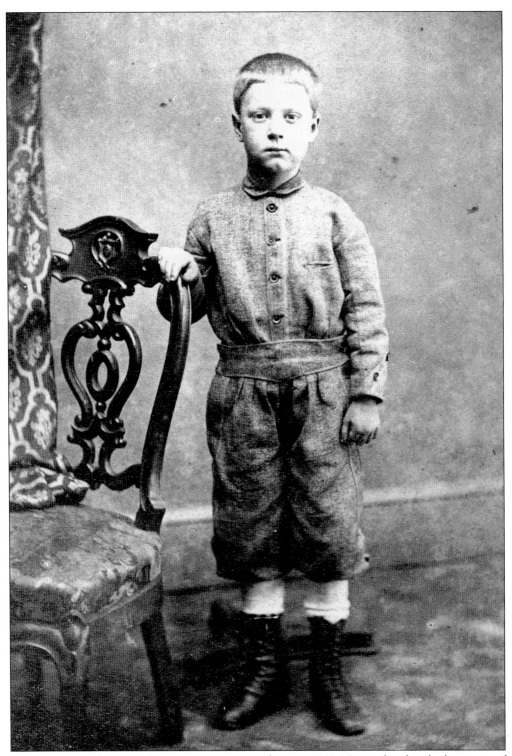

A boy poses for his portrait next to an ornate chair *c.* 1860. Notice his fine-looking suit of clothes and his laced boots. The name on the back of the portrait is J.L. Green.

Julius C. Hubbell was for many years the oldest lawyer in New York State. Born in 1788 in Lanesboro, Massachusetts, he married Anne Moore, daughter of Judge Pliny Moore, of Champlain, in 1812. He became a member of the bar in 1808. Over the years, he held various public offices, and in the 1840s, served a term as a member of the New York State legislature. He died in Chazy in 1880.

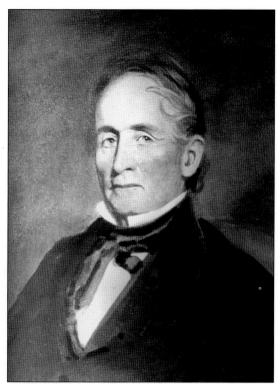

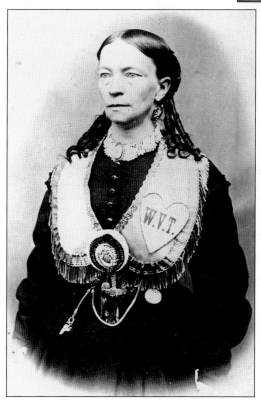

Jane Williams wears a serious look and a fringed wrap with a heart bearing the initials W.V.T. This photograph dates from c. 1870.

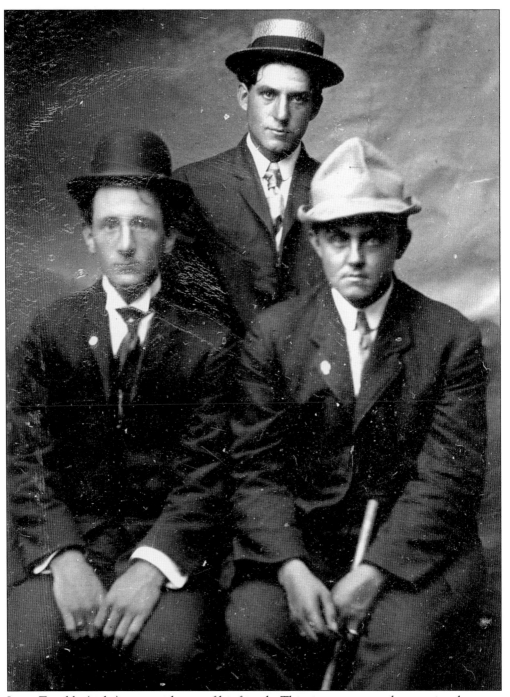

Louis Trombly (right) poses with two of his friends. This tintype was made sometime between the 1860s and the 1880s.

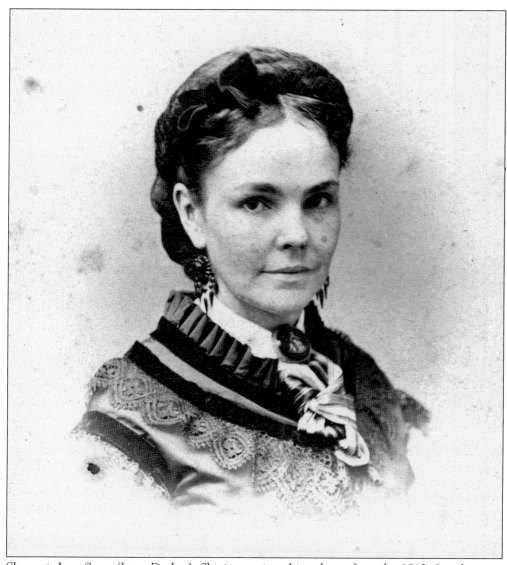

Shown is Jane Scott (later, Decker). She is mentioned in a letter from the 1840s found among the Hubbell papers. The letter is headed "Rules for Playing Jack Straws for the Special Guidance of the Young Ladies of Chazy and Vicinity." It reads as follows: "The Jack Straws must be held in an upright position in the hand resting upon the table. It is not considered fair either to drop them . . . or to open the hand so quickly . . . as to scatter them. . . . Two straws cannot be taken at once. . . . Any stirring of the straws after they are thrown . . . either by *dress, arm, fingers, hook, burls* is a violation. . . . Motion made by the breath . . . is an exception . . . except in cases of unnatural breathing such as sighs, intentional blowing, etc. . . . There by my side (this is confidential) sits Miss Hubbell and Mr. Wolf talking to me in such high praises of you all that really I can hardly identify one name unless it be Miss Scott. . . . Finally let me caution not to bite the hooking stick in two . . . especially . . . not to bite on the pin. Luckily I do not live in your part of the country, and Miss Hubbell is a mild tempered young lady, or I should expect to have my head bitten off for writing such an insinuating letter with these few remarks by way of commentary on the laws of the game of Jack Straws, I subscribe myself. Your very affectionate friend, Detsmilo D. Shricul."

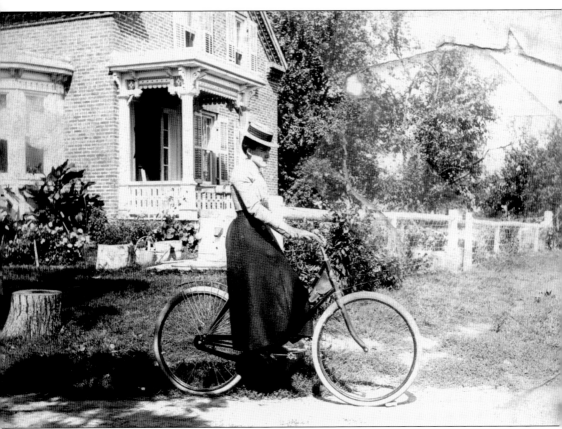

Daisy Bocare heads out on her bicycle c. the late 1800s. The people of Chazy love to hear a good yarn, and they have a saving and sharing nature. Born in 1877, Daisy Bocare Brunell of Lake Shore was an excellent storyteller who wrote down her memories for all to enjoy. In the following passage, she offers a few words about apples: "In front of my house is the site of the John LaFrambois house (1763). In front of his house was a monstrous apple tree. On this farm were loads of apple trees. Each fall the apple packers came and packed apples in barrels to be sold in New York City. At the same time plenty of apples were in bins in the cellar. None of the neighbors had apple trees. I remember the orchard—Greenings, Northern Spies, Fameuse, Pound Sweets and Bellflower. The Bellflower was the best apple I ever tasted—yellow right through. In the middle of the orchard was a Siberian Crab, which made the loveliest jelly and preserves. It's a mystery that we had the only apples in the neighborhood. I think Johnny Appleseed sprinkled some seeds as he passed. They claim this place was the first apple orchard." (Image, Daisy Baker.)

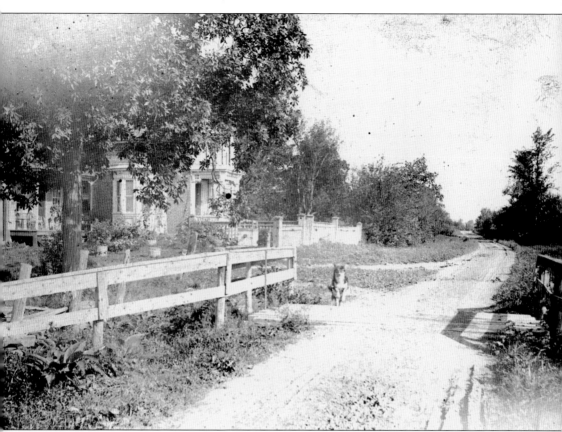

Shown is Lake Shore Road, where Daisy Bocare Brunell lived. She once wrote about a watch stolen in 1882: "One day when I was around five years old something happened which I have never forgotten. My folks didn't have a clock so they hung my father's large silver watch on the casing of the kitchen door. My mother, Aurelia, and I started out to get some early apples to make applesauce. The trees were in front of the Leazotte place. When we got back she looked to see the time and the watch was gone! She called my father, Albert, and the hired man and they at once got in touch with a few men in the neighborhood . . . Jacob Beaucaire, Sim Trombly, William D. Savage. . . . Someone said he had seen a man walking north along the road. The men each got on horseback and one man picked up a coil of rope. They went up Sheldon Lane and at the foot of the big hill they came upon the man walking along. Of course he was frightened and at first denied everything but when they told him they were going to hang him to a tree if he didn't produce the watch he at last gave up. They made the poor fellow get on his knees and beg—but at last they told him to start going and never show his face in these parts again." (Image, Daisy Baker.)

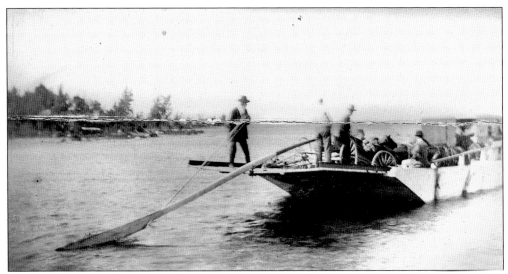

Shortly after the Civil War, Franklin Hill began running a ferry across Lake Champlain between Chazy Landing and Isle La Motte. Hill lived to be 90 and boasted that he had worn the same hat for 60 years. Mrs. Nelson Fisk and other women had their rugs washed by tying them with ropes to the ferry and letting them be towed across the lake. The picture above dates from *c.* 1890, and the one below from 1886. Winter ferry crossings are documented in the diary of William Saxe: "Friday Jan. 1, 1886—H.L. Carew died last night at 7:45 suddenly at L.J. Saxe. H. Ladd and I went for a casket to Plattsburgh with wagon. Got cloth covered one for $26.50. Dinner at Witherill House. Snow nearly gone. F.F. Chisholm & E. Hill watch tonight. Saturday Jan. 2, 1886—W.C. Hill sits up or sleeps at L.J. Saxes with corpse which was placed in casket this a.m. Drove colt on glare ice. Sunday Jan. 3, 1886—Very hard south wind all day skated H.L.C.'s body over lake—no crossing with horses. Funeral at M.E. Church. Rain at noon. Came back at 1:30. Monday Jan. 4, 1886—hard south wind—no crossing today. Ice poor. Tuesday Jan. 5, 1886—Rain and hard south wind. Wednesday Jan. 6, 1886—Wind N.W. Ice moved south & clear strip. Monday Jan. 11, 1886—Two teams cross today."

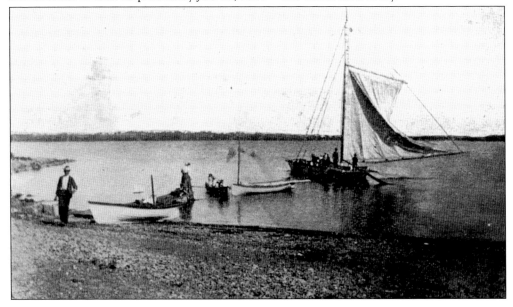

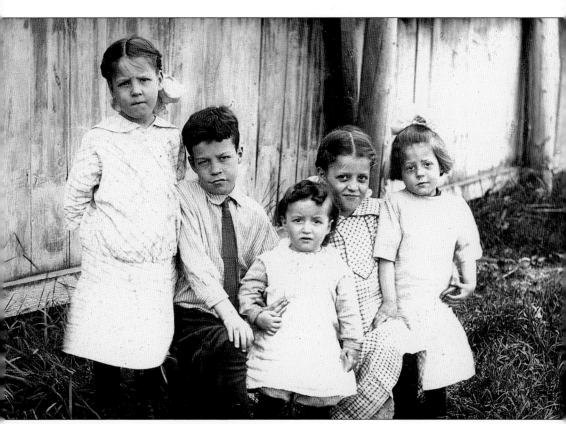

In front of a high fence, five children hold still long enough for this picture to be taken *c.* 1890. They do not appear too pleased with this interruption in their day.

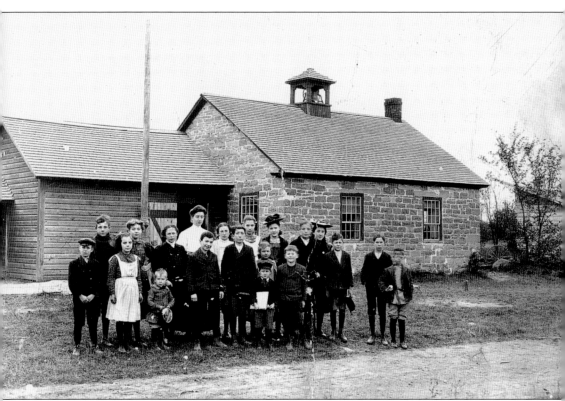

Pupils and their teacher pose outside the Old Stone School House *c.* the late 1890s. In her sketch entitled "An Honest Man," Daisy Bocare Brunell mentions a schoolmate: "When I was a young girl going to the red schoolhouse, there was a . . . girl there by the name of Mina Blow. They lived in a log house between the Bocares and the Robarges. Her father asked my father to lend him some money. I suppose it was for something to eat. Time went on and he didn't pay it back. One day my mother and I went to the sugar shanty with dinner for the men. When we got home there was a nice homemade rocking chair on the porch with a note pinned on it—'Mr. Bocare I couldn't pay you the money you lent me but I made you a chair.' My father went where they lived to thank them but they were gone. They could have easily slipped away without paying at all but the poor man did what he could. That chair stayed in our kitchen for years."

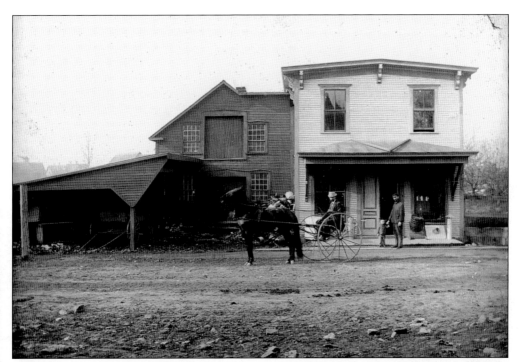

Fitch's Hall, named after a local tinsmith, Harrison Fitch, is pictured *c.* 1880. The building is located on the west side of Main Street.

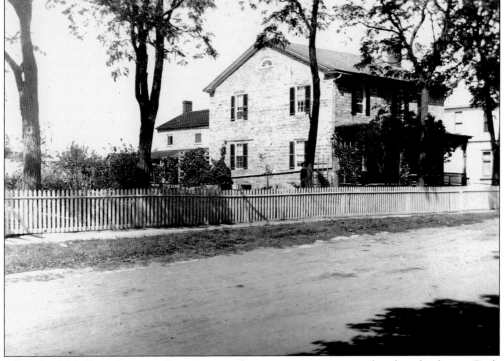

Julius C. Hubbell—a lawyer, a Democrat, and a state representative—lived in this house. Built *c.* 1820, the house is pictured in the late 1890s.

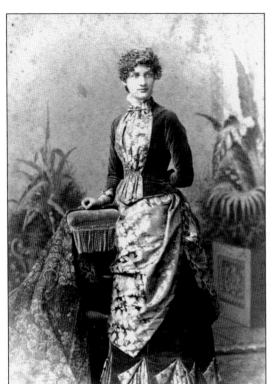

Cora Ladd Saxe is pictured on her wedding day in 1885. (Image, Helen Saxe Booth.)

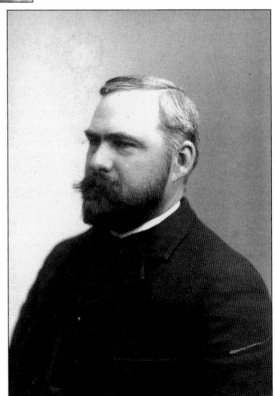

Dr. A.W. Fairbank set up his practice in Chazy in 1874 and continued working until his death in 1922. He is pictured c. 1890.

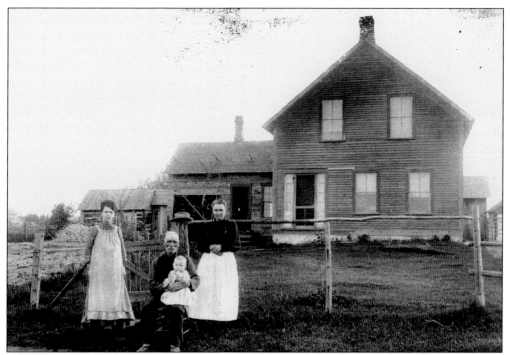

In this *c.* 1880 photograph, family members pose in front of their home in Sciota. (Image, Tim Neverett.)

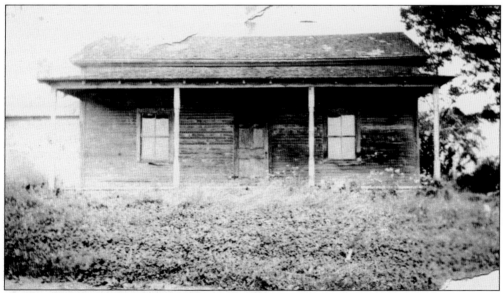

Shown *c.* the mid-1800s is the Matthew Douglas Saxe House. Matthew Saxe built a wharf so that the steamboat *Vermont* could dock and load or unload cargo. In 1809, his wharf was the only place at which the steamboat could dock. (Image, Jane Hess.)

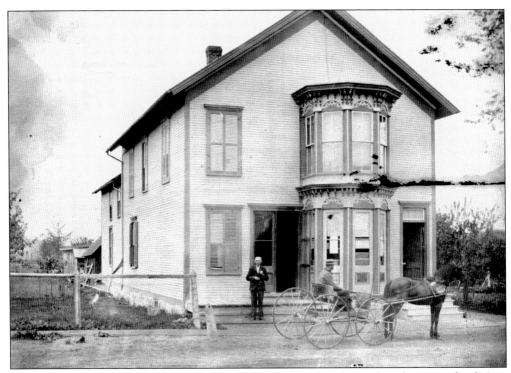

Henry Hinman ran a store and the post office from this building, located on the west side of Main Street. Pictured c. 1890, the building now serves as a private residence. (Image, Daisy Baker.)

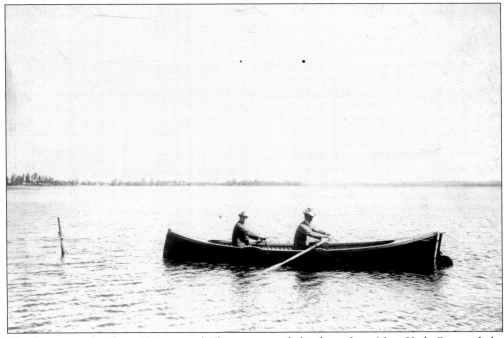

The Stevenson brothers, George and Thomas, rowed this boat from New York City to Lake Champlain c. 1900. George was a dentist in Chazy and West Chazy. (Image, Daisy Baker.)

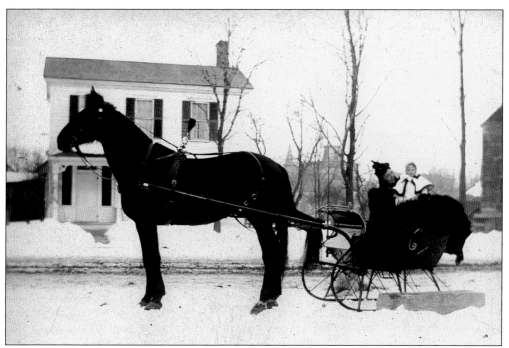

Out for a winter's ride in the sleigh *c.* 1895 are "Auntie Peg" Houghton (wife of S.A. Houghton) and Katherine Seymour.

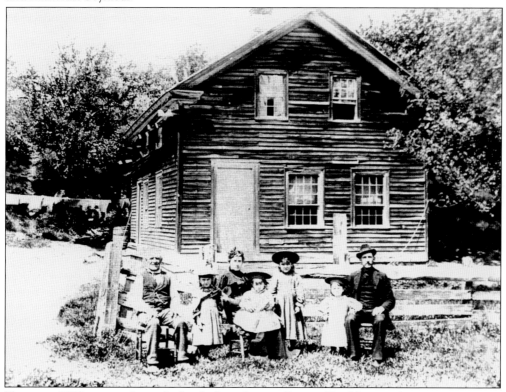

Shown *c.* 1880 are members of a family from Sciota. (Image, Tim Neverett.)

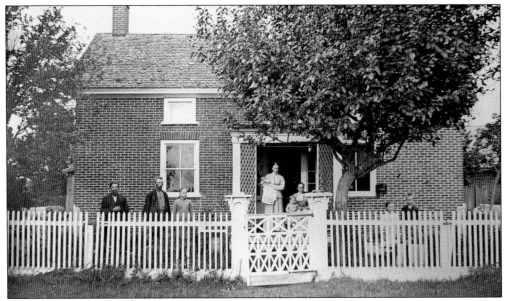

The nine people gathered outside Michael Hay's farmhouse c. 1882 are identified, from left to right, as William McGibson, Michael Hay, Cora, Lillian, Almina, Hannah du Boise Hay, Rhoda, Eunice, and Clarence D. Hay.

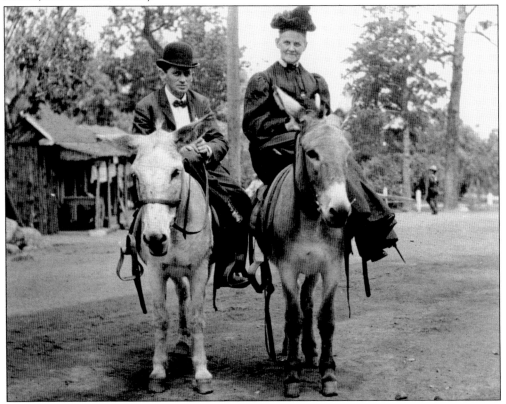

David and Deborah Harris are going out for a ride. The photograph was taken in West Chazy c. 1900. (Image, David Martin.)

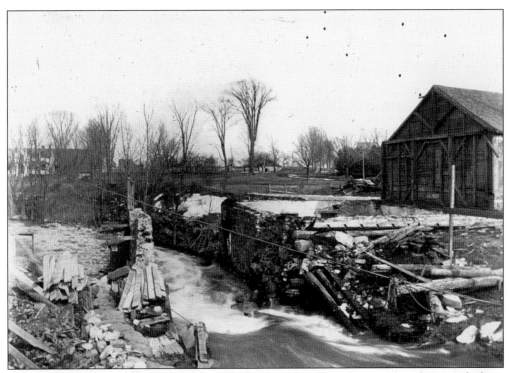

The Grant Douglas Mill was located on the bank of the Chazy River. This photograph dates from c. 1850. A fire station now occupies this site.

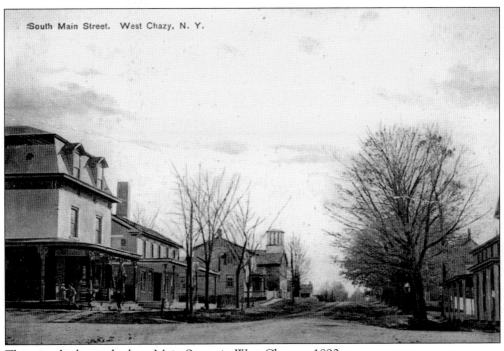

South Main Street. West Chazy, N. Y.

This view looks south along Main Street in West Chazy c. 1890.

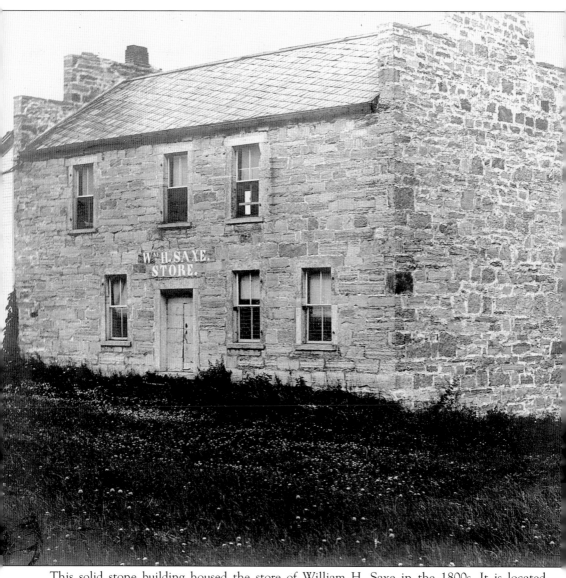

This solid stone building housed the store of William H. Saxe in the 1800s. It is located at Chazy Landing.

Two

1900–1929

The village of West Chazy is remarkable for the beauty and variety of its architecture. Houses range from a simple wooden dwelling built by William Lawrence in 1819 (probably the oldest remaining house in the village) to the cluster of buildings erected in the boom years of 1913–1915.

The classic Federal-style house built by Samuel Bayley for Putnam Lawrence in 1832, the earlier 1827 Stephen Atwood house, and the stone Hedding house of the mid-1830s represent a simple, dignified early period. Other examples of this style include a brick house built by Asa Stiles during the same period and the brick building that was once the Wesleyan Methodist parsonage, built in the 1840s. The brick home that was once a Catholic nunnery and the structure that once served as the Methodist parsonage likewise date from the 1840s. Two homes are built with locally quarried Chazy limestone. It is probable that the brick houses are made from Beekmantown brick.

A more elaborate 1840s brick house with a beautiful stoop and doorway in the neoclassical style is the Orson Hedding house. Hiding under modern siding is its twin (without the Neoclassic entrance), a dwelling built by Orville K. Wood next to the bridge on what is now Route 22.

Reflecting a period of more ornamental tastes are the brick Italianate villa known as the O'Brien house (built c. 1860 by O.K. Wood's brother Victor A. Wood) and the mansard-roofed Amasa B. Wood house (erected in the spring of 1878).

The former West Chazy railroad station, now a private residence, is an exceptionally fine piece of architecture. It was constructed in 1907, the year after the quaint Dodge Library (sporting its own mansard roof) was built in 1906. Another attractive public building is the West Chazy Elementary School, a neo-Georgian school built in 1933–1934.

Perhaps the biggest architectural explosion in the village began in 1913, when Maude Lawson ordered a house from the Sears and Roebuck catalog. The prefabricated pieces, complete even to the nails and paint, were delivered by freight train to the West Chazy station and carted up the hill to a site on West Church Street. The next year, H.D. Carlton ordered a similar house from the Chicago Molding and Milling Company. The pieces of this house were carried to Route 22 by the dam in the Little Chazy River. It was put up in 1914–1915. At the same time, a gift from Loyal Smith, the well-proportioned Wesleyan Methodist brick church, with its adjoining parsonage, was erected near the school and library.

Lewis Emery, the first professional well driller in West Chazy, bought a lot and, c. 1914, built the interesting cobblestone house on Route 22. A year or two later, the similar cobblestone house was built immediately south.

—David Martin

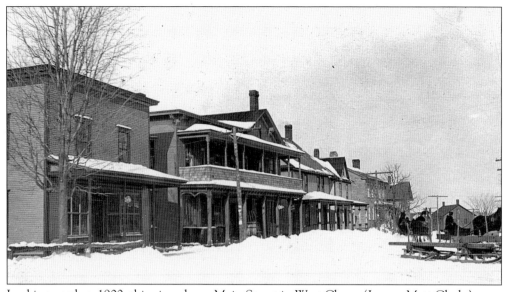

Looking north *c*. 1900, this view shows Main Street in West Chazy. (Image, Matt Clark.)

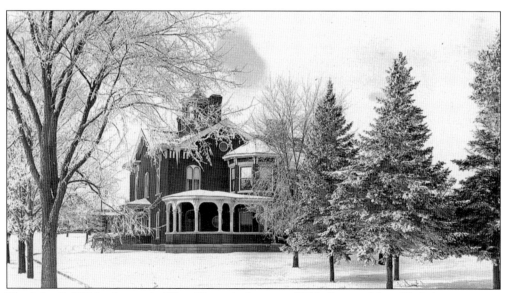

The John F. O'Brien house, in West Chazy, is shown *c*. 1900. (Image, Matt Clark.)

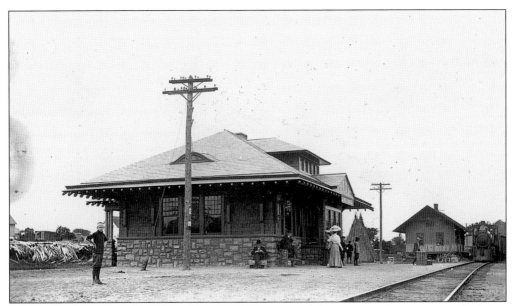

Pictured *c.* 1907 is the West Chazy train station. The previous station can be seen in the background.

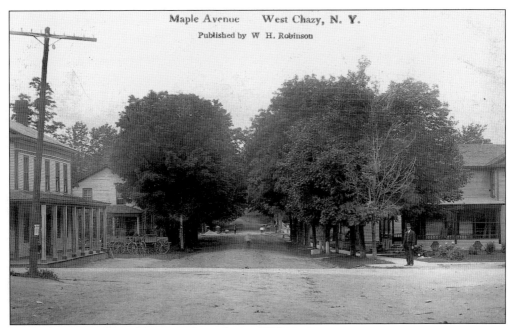

Maple Avenue in West Chazy is seen in this *c.* 1900 view.

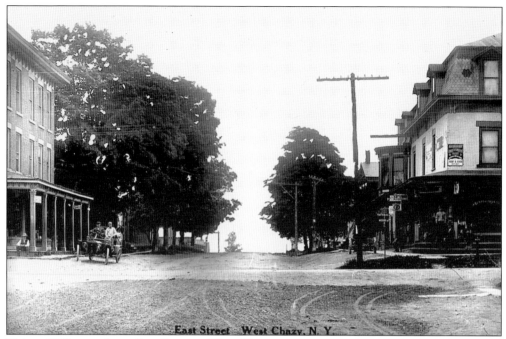

This *c*. 1910 view shows East Street in West Chazy.

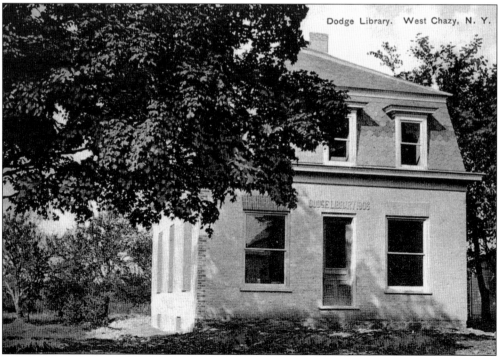

The Dodge Library, in West Chazy, is pictured in 1906.

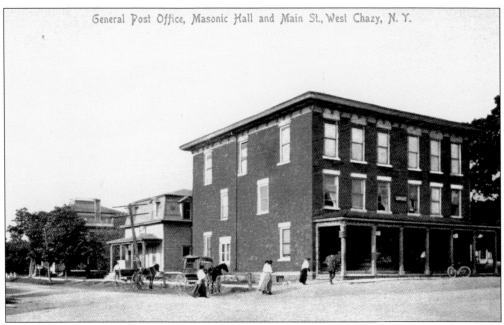

The Robinson store, in West Chazy, is shown in 1906. (Image, David Martin.)

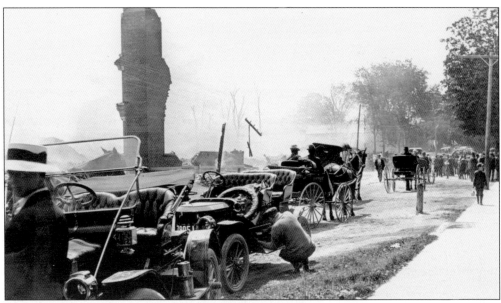

On June 30, 1912, the Robinson store burned, nearly destroying the entire village of West Chazy. The cause of the fire was unknown. H.S. Bruso's store and home, across the street, were also destroyed. (Image, David Martin.)

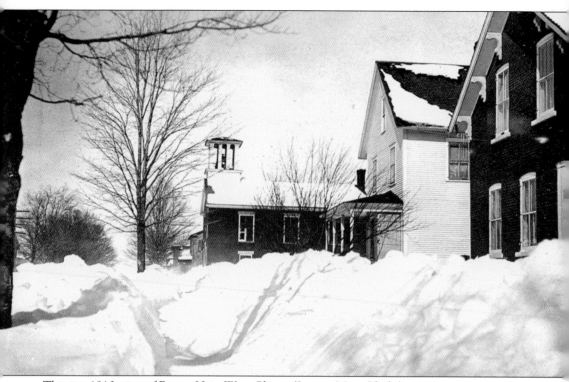

This is a 1910 view of Route 22 in West Chazy. (Image, Matt Clark.)

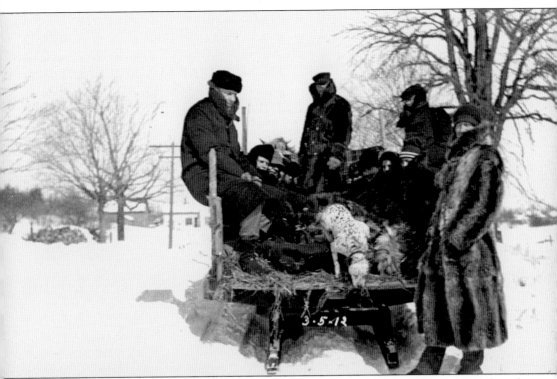

West Chazy residents enjoy a sleigh ride in 1912. Each man was taxed according to the value of his farm but, instead of paying money, would work it out. The road commissioner would keep track of the time each person worked and credit it to his tax. The men would fasten a plow to the back of a sleigh and plow one way and then turn around and plow the other side. When it was impossible to plow the road, they would take to the field. In those days, there were no automobiles. John Brunell was head of the road gang, and while the horses rested, the men would come into the house and play cards. The taxes on both the Brunell farms were about $40. (Information, Daisy Brunell; image, David Martin.)

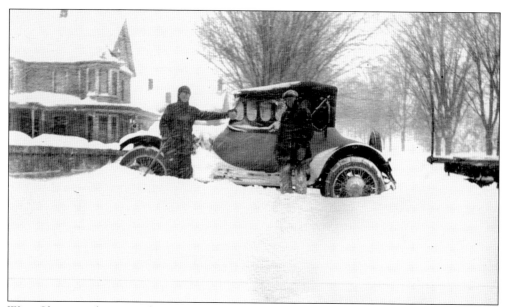

West Chazy residents are shown outside the Richardson House after the snowstorm of 1917. (Image, David Martin.)

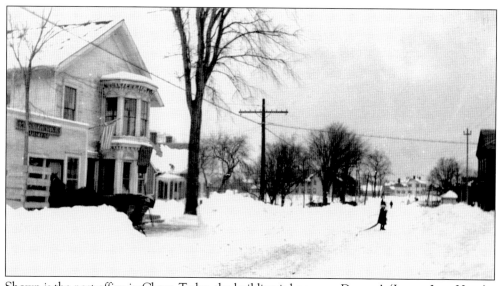

Shown is the post office in Chazy. Today, the building is known as Dumars'. (Image, Jane Hess.)

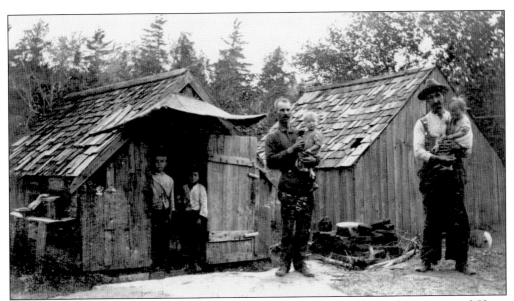

By 1900, blueberries had become a major commercial crop in the Flat Rock area, west of Chazy in the town of Altona (part of the town of Chazy until 1857). The Wood brothers had a portion of the Flat Rock area, with shelters, where the pickers lived. They set up a temporary store for selling the goods and accepting and crating the berries. At night, the berries were delivered to the West Chazy railroad station to be immediately shipped. Pickers came from quite a distance, among them the Cawganawaga Indians. The chief always came with them but would pick no berries. Young Ben Sullivan worked for Lester A. Childs, who bought the berries from the Wood brothers or the pickers and shipped them. Pictured are families who lived and worked on the Rock during berry season. All parts of the shelters were numbered for removal in the winter and setup in the spring. (Information, Nell Sullivan; image, David Martin.)

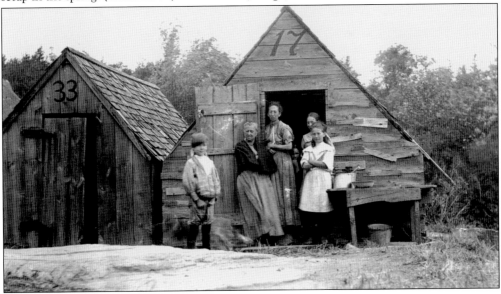

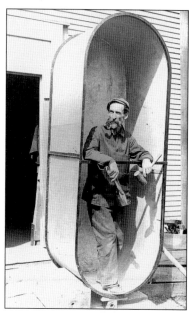

A man works on a water trough in West Chazy *c.* 1910. (Image, Matt Clark.)

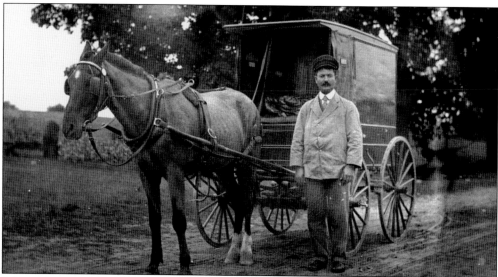

John Michael peddles goods from his wagon *c.* 1900. Daisy Bocare Brunell recalls a meat peddler named Prisque Patnode, who came from Cooperville and settled in Chazy *c.* 1910: "He was the most accommodating man I ever knew. . . . We bought meat from him for years. If we had the money all right, if we didn't . . . we would pay when we were ready. When my husband died, I knew we owed him. My husband, John, had sold him a cow with the understanding that we would buy our meat from him and let it go toward the sale of the cow. After a while I went to settle up with him. . . . He said he . . . had a book in which he kept his accounts although he could neither read or write. That book was a curious one . . . One place a picture was drawn of a church—that meant Father Victor's account, another had a hat with feathers—that meant Mrs. Mossey the milliner, another was a rat with a long tail—that was Fred Ratta's account. I looked through the book but could not find a trace of my debt. . . . We agreed on a small sum and I would pay for the meat I bought from him hereafter. It would have been a crime to cheat a trusting old man like that."

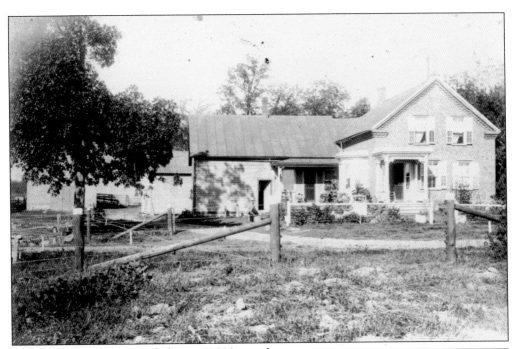

The Brunell home, pictured above *c.* 1910, stood on Lake Shore Road in Chazy. Daisy Brunell, shown below at age three, stands outside in November 1918. She recalled, "A funny thing happened years ago when the children were all home. A couple of the boys and Edith and Mary (Gonya) went to spend the evening at their Uncle Robert's, a short distance from us. During the evening who comes but two men with their threshing machine. We had expected them to do our threshing later in the week but their coming unexpectedly made me find them a place to sleep. We were a large family (11) and the beds were nearly all occupied. . . . The first room as you go upstairs was Edith and Mary's room. I decided to place [Edith and Mary] somewhere else and give the two men that bed . . . sure that I would be awake when they came home to tell them of the change but they stayed longer than I expected and . . . I fell asleep. When the girls came home they . . . carefully crept upstairs so I wouldn't know they had stayed so late. They both got undressed in the dark. . . . Edith got ready first and groped her way to find the bed when suddenly she came in contact with a big mustache. She let out a scream, which woke up the household. After some explaining I got everyone settled for the night. . . . We laughed about this incident for years." (Image, Daisy Baker.)

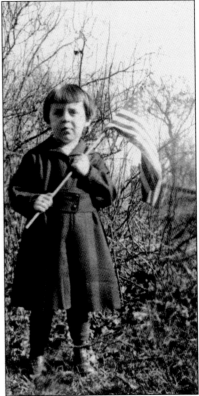

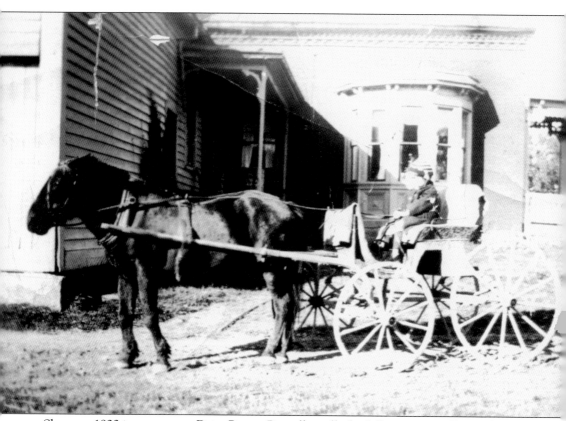

Shown c. 1922 is a pony cart. Daisy Bocare Brunell recalls the following story: "It was the spring of the year and before the hard road went through. This day the roads were very bad. It being Monday we were busy with washing and housecleaning. All of a sudden I looked out and saw Father Victor and Bishop Conroy drive into the yard. Father Victor had driven his car as far as the road would allow, and wanting to take the Bishop to his camp a mile or so down the road asked to borrow a horse and wagon. As it happened the men were all working on the road with all the horses so there was only the Shetland pony and the pony cart left. At once Father Victor said that would be all right so Eva hitched the pony to the cart and those two big men got in with Father Victor driving. The pony started on the gallop as he always did. It was a sight to be remembered to see those two big men on a seat meant for children. Pretty soon they came back with the Bishop driving and somehow managed to turn into the yard without upsetting. I believe the pony must have been glad that the trip was over. It's too bad we didn't have a camera to take their picture as they drove into the yard. I heard later that the Bishop enjoyed his ride very much." (Image, Daisy Baker.)

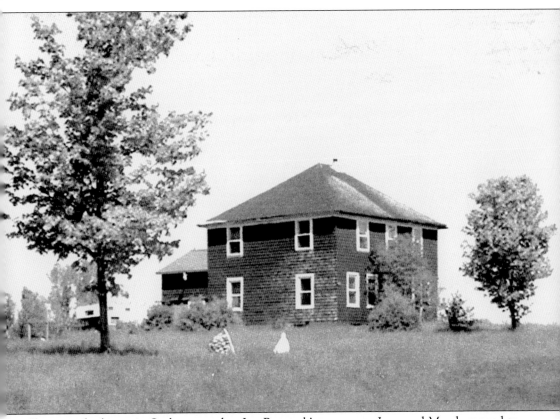

Shown is the house in Suckortown that Joe Barcomb's two mares June and Maude moved to West Chazy in the early 1900s. George Deno recalls, "A man by the name of Joe Barcomb had the unfortunate experience of watching his home burn to the ground. He needed a home so, instead of rebuilding, he went to Suckortown and acquired a house. The house had originally been begun in the Chazy village behind where Harry Barber lived. Joseph Laramie III bought the partially completed house and moved it to Suckortown, where he had it rebuilt south of the river and west of the Minkler Road. When William H. Miner was having the dam built, he wanted the spot for his project. Miner purchased the house and gave it to Joseph Barcomb, providing Barcomb would move it. The distance between Suckortown and West Chazy is about 10 miles. Barcomb used his two mares—June, who was white, and Maude, a bay—and his wagon. No one knows how long this took, but he managed to get all the pieces to the appointed spot. Barcomb then invited his neighbors over for a house raising. A man by the name of Ben Bruce lived in the house from the 1920s to the 1980s. The house still stands to this day, somewhat crookedly, on the Ketchum Bridge Road in West Chazy."

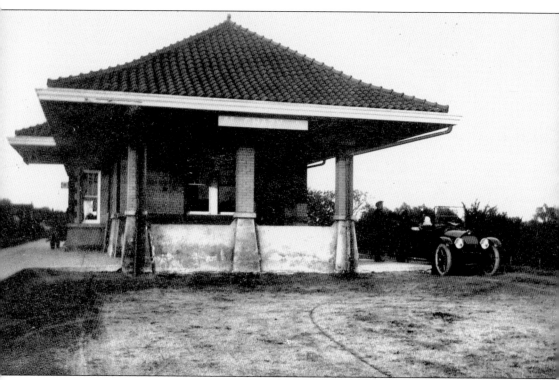

The Chazy station is shown as it appeared in 1911. Virginia DeGray remembers, "Edmund Ducharme (November 7, 1890–September 13, 1973) formerly from 1 Bison Road (Old Miner Farm Road) Chazy, was employed by the Delaware & Hudson Railroad. When the Chazy work crew merged with West Chazy work crew, Ducharme acquired the responsibility of taking care of the Chazy area in addition to working with the West Chazy crew. The Chazy work crew reported to work at the car house, which also was where the railroad handcars were stored. Freight trains would stop on the second track behind the Ducharmes' house. Alice and Pauline remember how their mother, Albertine, would feed and give water to the hobos who would ride in the boxcars. Pauline remembers that, if the shades were down in the house, the hobos would keep on walking. If the shades were up, they would knock on the door, and Albertine Ducharme would feed them on the back steps."

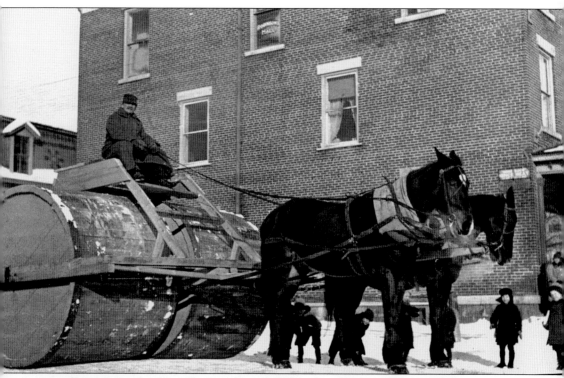

A snow roller is pictured in West Chazy in the early 1900s. Guy Cassevaugh recalls this story: "Many times down through the years I have remembered with a laugh my father's c. 1917 invention—but it worked. It must have been sometime during World War I, because I can remember it and I am now 73. In those days, winters in the rural town of West Chazy were very snowy and the roads weren't plowed like they are today. Instead, the landowners used huge wooden rollers drawn by a team of horses packed the snow down. Of course, there were very few cars. People got around with a cutter and horse, just like in the Currier and Ives prints. We had moved to town and sold the horse. My father missed his cutter. Then, he had a great idea. He took a farm sleigh, which consists of two sleds hitched together, one in back of the other, with a big box on the top. The front sled was movable. He bolted a one-cylinder motor from a motorboat inside the box. It was belted to a big wooden wheel about three feet in circumference into which he drove big spikes about six inches apart. The wheel hung between the runners on the back sled. I helped him build it, as I was his only son. The machine had a steering wheel on the front sled with ropes that ran to each front-runner. My father stood in the box and with the ropes and directed the front sled either to the left or to the right, as he desired. There was one drawback to the "sleighmobile" though. Every time we crossed the railroad tracks, some of the spikes would break off. We spent a lot of time replacing them and trying to avoid the railroad tracks. My father's machine was a big attraction in the small town of West Chazy; it also was a very noisy one and much disliked by the horses who reared and snorted at the smelly contraption. I always say my father built the first version of the snowmobile." (Image, David Martin.)

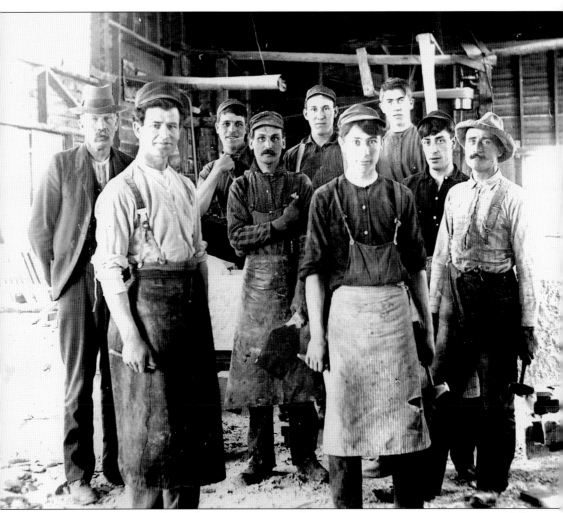

Men pause during their workday at the West Chazy Granite Company *c.* 1900. From left to right are William Carnes, Ernest LeBlond, Bert Cassevaugh, Joseph Cassevaugh, Andrew Lutz, Albert LaBounty, Fred Carnes, Harry LaBounty, and Noah Brunell.

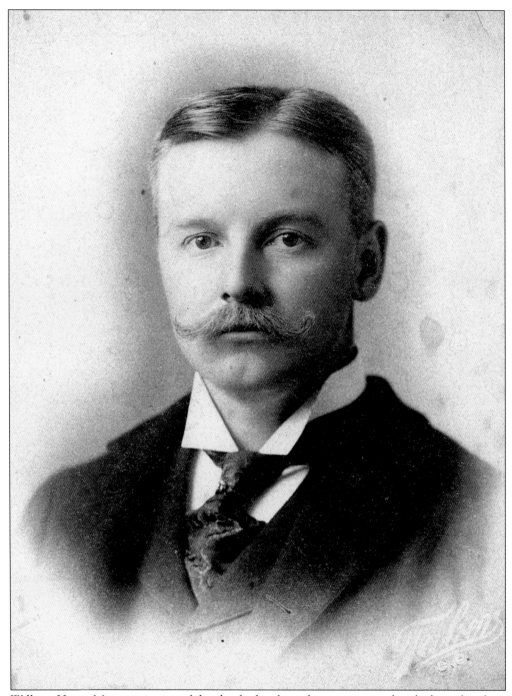

William Henry Miner, inventor of the shock absorbing device associated with the railroad car coupler still in use today, was a major figure in Chazy. He is pictured as a young man.

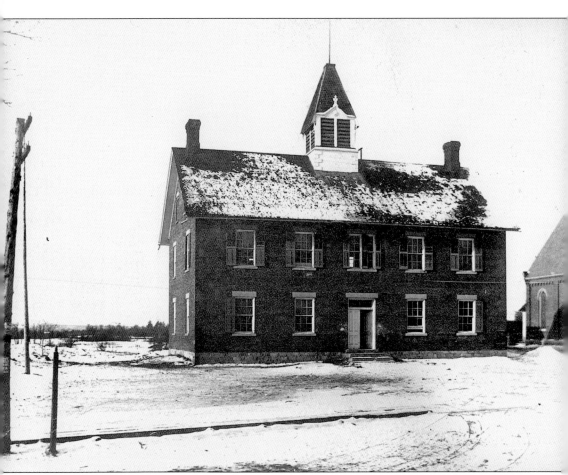

This is the original schoolhouse in Chazy village, located where Gray Gables stands today. The picture dates from 1874. Ralph Pombrio recalls, "I was born in Sciota on September 16, 1909. I attended a two-room school located at Obers Corners. The school was the usual rural school for those days—a box stove for heat, a pail of water with a dipper from which everyone drank, the usual outhouses as toilets. About midday, we had recess, with no supervision for our play period. When I was in the sixth grade, a teacher was employed who was very stern but fair and kind. During the winter months she taught us to square dance and danced with us in the hallway between the two rooms. When the weather permitted, she taught us ball games and other sports in the schoolyard. In short, she had a sincere interest in each of us. She taught 25 to 30 students in grades five, six, seven, and eight. It was at this time that I decided to become a teacher, even though she never spoke to any of us about any vocation nor did she ever know how she impressed me."

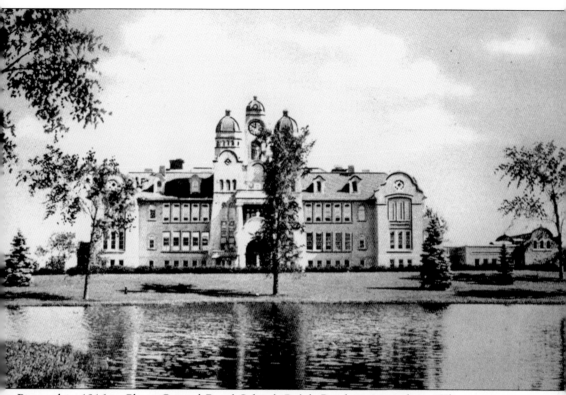

Pictured in 1916 is Chazy Central Rural School. Ralph Pombrio remembers, "There was no high school in our area. The great inventor and philanthropist William H. Miner had built Chazy Central Rural School in 1916, but our school district in Sciota was not part of this centralization and was six miles away. I made an appointment with Louise Inglis, the principal of Chazy Central, and I was accepted as a student for the fall of 1924. Immediately, I had to solve the problem of those six miles. My parents were cooperative, but they had no financial means to assist me. I had to pay as much as $2.50 per week for my ride to school. I had to get work the prior summer and every summer afterwards to earn this money."

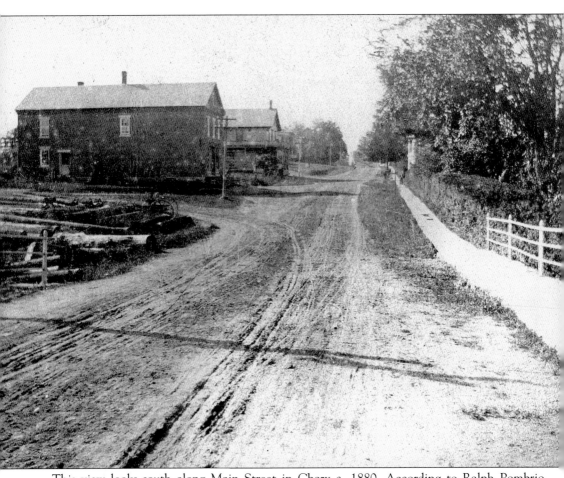

This view looks south along Main Street in Chazy c. 1880. According to Ralph Pombrio, "Chazy village had little or no electricity. William H. Miner spent a small fortune trying to make a dam in Chazy Lake. The ground was porous and could never be made to work as a source of waterpower. Miner then moved his enterprise to the Great Chazy River and constructed two powerhouses in Altona. These were connected by a six-foot-diameter pipe called a penstock. The powerhouses became a huge success. A 22,000-volt power line was run to Heart's Delight Farm (the Miner's residence). Thence, it was transmitted in lower voltage to light up the village of Chazy and the Presbyterian and the Catholic churches."

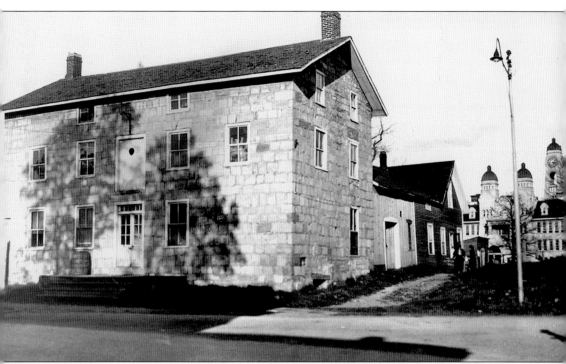

This 1917 photograph shows Scott's Store in Chazy in 1917, with the Chazy School in the background. Ralph Pombrio recalls, "The library was used as study hall. During one of my periods there, I was looking up the Babylonians for my history class assignment. A voice at my side said, 'What are you looking up?' I turned and saw William H. Miner at my side. I told him my assignment, to which he replied, 'What is happening there now?' I said, 'I don't know,' for in those days, there were no televisions, radios, and few newspapers. He responded, 'There is no need looking into past events unless you associate them with the present.' I never forgot his sage thought; I graduated from Chazy Central Rural School in 1928."

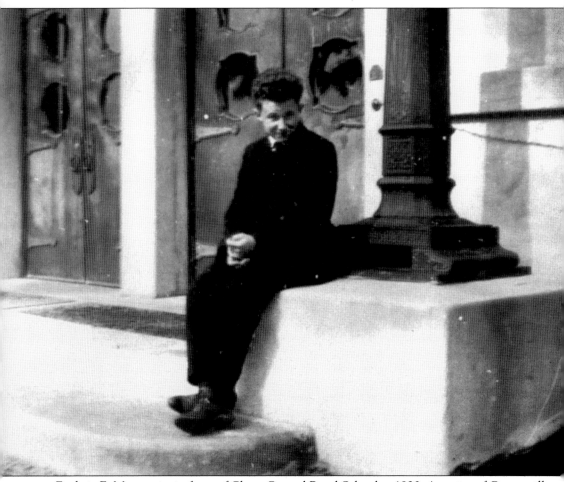

Frederic E. Mooers sits in front of Chazy Central Rural School c. 1920. A native of Cooperville (where his father operated a country store near the Chazy River Bridge), Mooers was 10 years old in the fall of 1916, when he entered fifth grade at Chazy Central Rural School. He started his first day by dancing along an eight-inch plank over an open ditch and reaching a doorway on the north side of the school, with construction still in progress. Chazy was then a busy trading center for people around the area. (Information, Robert Booth; image, Frederic E. Mooers.)

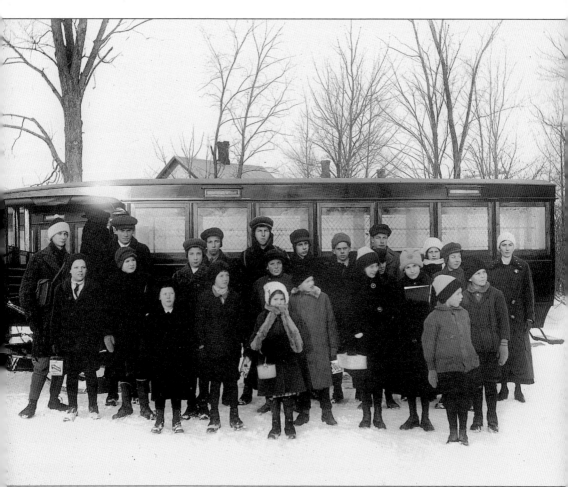

Bundled up for winter, some two dozen Chazy Central Rural School students stand alongside their horse-drawn school bus *c.* 1920. Part of the education plan was that all students were to be bused from the countryside to the school. At first, this was done with long horse-drawn carriages built to carry many children—on wheels in good weather but in covered sleighs in the winter. In 1916, automobiles were increasingly common, but only present Routes 9 and 9B were somewhat paved. All back roads were gravel or dirt and not well maintained. The busing program worked well in good weather but not so well on snow-covered roads with drifts and not at all during mud season. In the cold weather, a charcoal-burning stove was located under the driver's seat to heat the sleigh, and the passengers were wrapped in robes. Frederic E. Mooers recalls that a robe once caught fire. No real harm was done, but there was much excitement. Mooers's father claimed that he had a "vision" about a fire the night before. (Information, Robert Booth.)

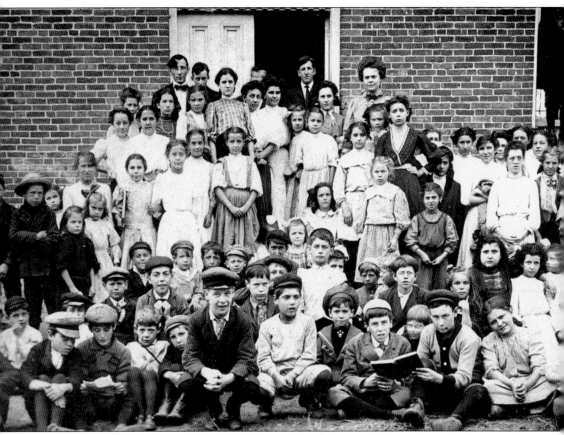

Children pose in front of the Old Chazy School, located where Grey Gables is today. A route from Cooperville to Chazy (about five miles) was along the present Stetson Road, the Sarachan Road, and Route 9. The road sloped down toward the railroad crossing at the Sarachan intersection. One day, bus driver Lem North lost control of the converted carriage-sleigh, which tipped over at the tracks. The passengers were thrown around inside, the horses panicked and became entangled, and North suffered a leg injury that lasted the rest of his life. Then, a train approached. Thankfully, the engineer was able to stop and the crew gave help. The students were loaded in the caboose and taken to the Chazy train station and, from there, to school. During the mud season and when winter roads were drifted in, open horse-drawn farm wagons became buses. The five-mile trip could not be completed comfortably without a warmup break. Thus, a stop was made at the Poland home on Dixon Road, where students warmed themselves in the kitchen before moving on to school. (Information, Robert Booth; image, Frederic E. Mooers.)

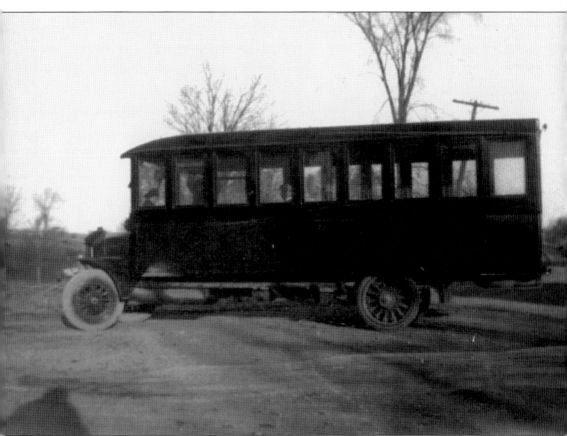

Shown is a Pierce Arrow school bus *c. 1920*. By the time Frederic E. Mooers graduated from high school, the roads and buses had improved. The school system then rolled along on the pneumatic tires of handsome Pierce Arrow buses. Mooers says that he "sure worked hard for his education." (Information, Robert Booth; image, Frederic E. Mooers.)

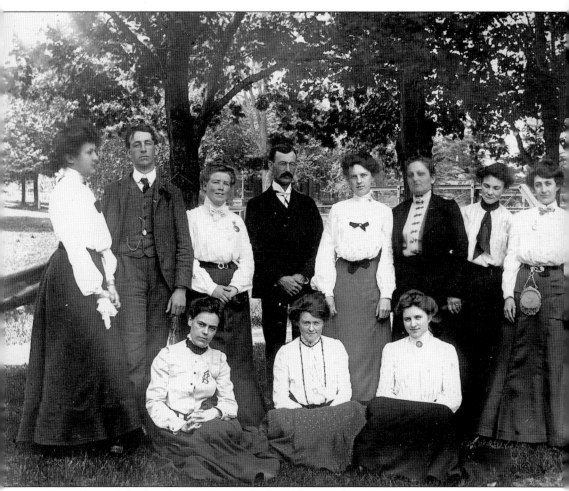

Members of the Teachers Institute of West Chazy gather *c.* 1910. Among those pictured are Mrs. Sweet, Mr. FitzPatrick, Nell Barnett, Ruth Taylor, and Kate Algie.

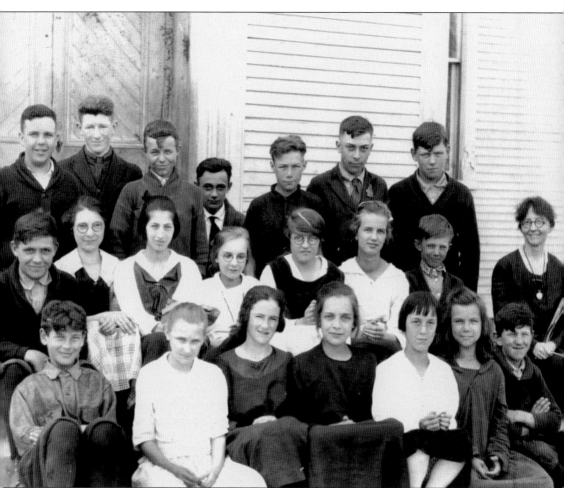

West Chazy students pose for a class picture in 1922. From left to right are the following: (front row) Janice Brown, Mildred Robare, Frances Harvey, Gertrude LaBounty, Morgan Clark, Margarite LaMay, and Hubert Jennette; (middle row) Earl Beeman, Mary Powers, Shirley Goodale, Lillian Stone, Marion Starks, Adelide Carlton, Ernest Scribner, and Edith Junior (teacher); (back row) Clifford Weeden, Arthur Harvey, Joseph LaMay, George Lucia, Roy Landry, Herbert Chauvin, and Francis Atwood. (Image, Kim Neverett Howley.)

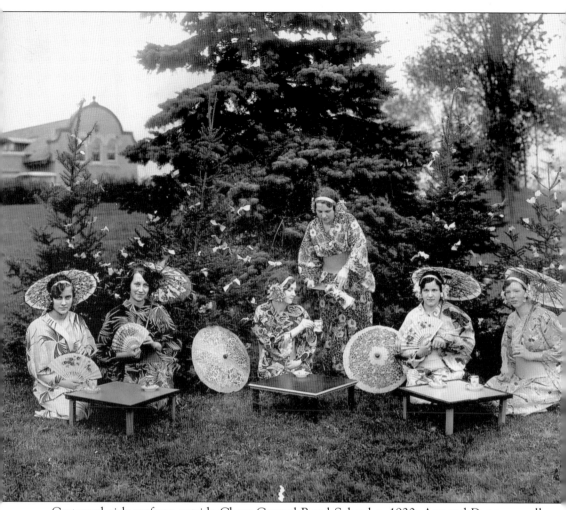

Costumed girls perform outside Chazy Central Rural School *c.* 1920. Armand Duprey recalls that his father, Leeward Duprey (born in 1900), started to work at the new school sometime in 1915. Leeward would work a 12-hour shift in the boiler room every day, with one day off a month for a wage of $75 per month. Two men worked the 24-hour day; so, when the day off came, the man on would have to work a double shift. This changed in 1930, when new laws came in for the eight-hour day. The boilers heated several buildings, including the school, and when it was minus 20 degrees during the night and very cold during the days, 44 tons of coal would be used in three days—all shoveled into the boilers by hand (22 tons per man). When the chief engineer, a Mr. Tall, retired, the job went to Leeward Duprey. The Dupreys lived in one of the nine-room apartments on the sixth floor of the school. Armand Duprey's grandfather George Brown never learned to read or write but could play a tune on his violin after listening to it just two or three times. Brown never had a job away from home. He cut wood, sold fish, hunted, and played violin for dances. (Information, Bob Cheeseman.)

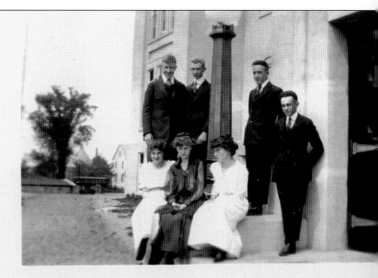

Chazy Central Rural School's class of 1918 included John Pike, Harold Davenport, Viola Nordin, Dorothy Hyde, Lucy Heaton, Talbot Dressin, and Carl Mooers. (Image, Helen Saxe Booth.)

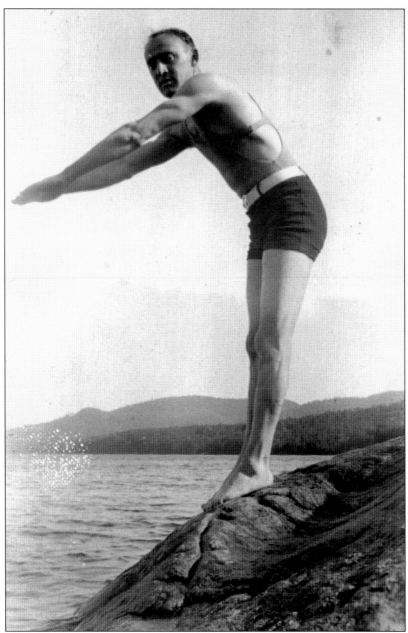

While building the new Chazy school in 1916, William H. Miner commissioned talented sculptor John Rae, whose studio stood where the Beekmantown School is today, to create two statues: an idealized female for the girls' swimming pool and a young man for the boys' pool. Rae noticed a young man working out at the Plattsburgh YMCA, which had been built a few years before through the generosity of Loyal L. Smith of West Chazy. Rae asked the man, Myron "Mickey" Caplan, age 20 at the time, if he would be willing to pose for the male statue. Caplan agreed, and Rae made a series of sketches from which he modeled the statue. The statue was cast in bronze and placed by the boys' pool in the new school c. 1918. Caplan's son, Irving Caplan of Malone, says Rae captured an excellent likeness of his father. Who the female model was is not known. (Information, David Martin; image, Irving Caplan.)

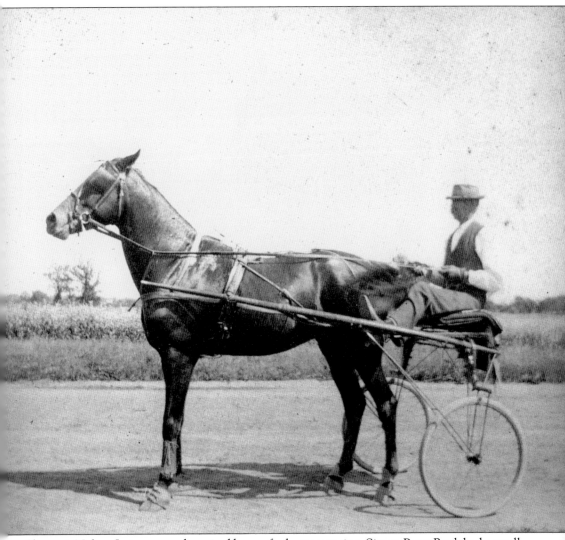

Shown is Nelson Latremore, who raised horses for harness racing. Simon Peter Rock had a small potato farm in Chazy, which is in the Latremore family today. His grandson Conrad Heaton would visit him and remembers Grandpa Rock letting him ride on the "stone boat," a heavy wooden sled pulled by horses, to haul stones out of the fields—quite a thrill for a boy, according to Mary Louise Rock. He would feel like a king surveying the countryside. When construction projects were under way on the lakeshore, Simon Peter Rock would haul the stones to the job site and sell them. He spoke both French and English. However, he felt that it would be best to Americanize the name, so the spelling of the family's last name changed from Roque to Rock between 1897 and 1908. At Christmastime, William H. Miner gave a party for all the children at Harmony Hall, a beautiful building on the Miner Farm, and the Rock family's present was a box of chocolates. (Information, J. Daniel Sullivan Jr.)

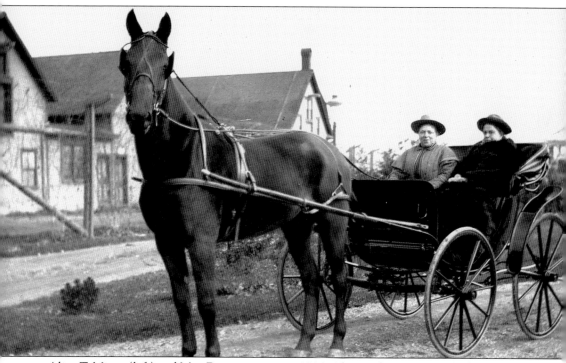

Alice T. Miner (left) and Mrs. Dunn are seen in 1906. Alice and W.H. Miner had many visitors at their farm outside Chazy village, a farm named Heart's Delight. One of their visitors left behind a poem entitled "The Garden of Heart's Delight."

I dream of a garden of flowers
On the bank of a cool river laid.
Of wide spreading fields, abundant in yields,
Encircled by mountains blue shade.

A glory of woodland, pine, maple and birch
With the flickering sunlight between.
Where the cell of the birds in God's Infinite Church
Makes harmony whole and serene.

I dream of a garden of sunshine
In beauty all drenched from above,
Where pansy or rose meeting larkspur's tall blow
Thrive in perfection of love.

Where the trees and the vines and the lilacs blow
With a loveliness rich and rare,
For flowering shrub or lupine bud
Are tended with loving care.

I dream of a valley of roving life
Where sheep with undisturbed right,
And buffalo, deer and elk without fear
Graze the pastures of Heart's Delight.
On hill, field and slope, God is the hope
And at evening bell's soft vesper call,
The cares of day are folded away
And gentle peace reigns over all.

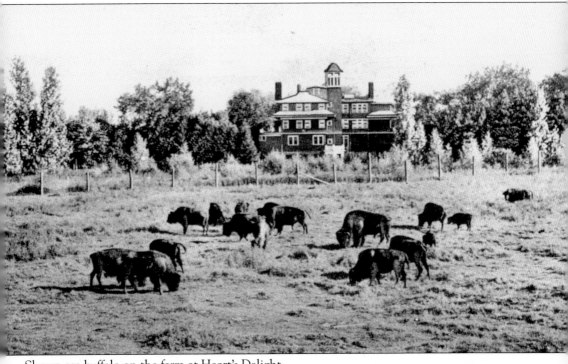

Shown are buffalo on the farm at Heart's Delight.

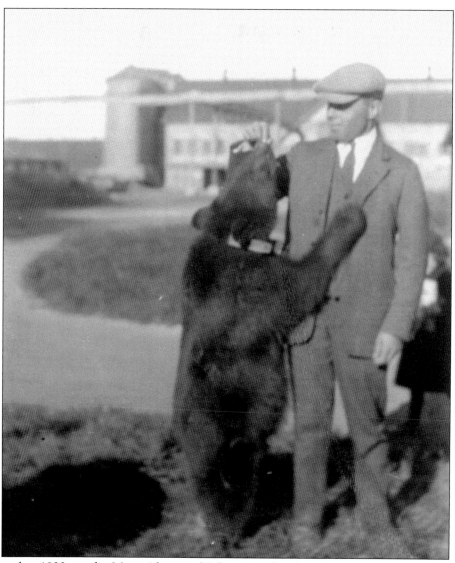

Pictured *c.* 1920 are the Miners' bear and Johnny Maslowski. The first bear was a male cub about the size of a full-grown cat. Mr. Senell, a laborer at the Miner farm, first saw him in the poultry yard in a wire cage. Senell was walking by this yard when he heard a whining and crying. Investigating further, he discovered the cub chewing at the wire to free himself. His mouth was bleeding from the effort. After a few days, he was transported to the Flat Rock and placed in an enclosure near the fish hatchery. This became his permanent home. At two years of age, he was full grown, fat, slick, and beautiful. He weighed about 300 pounds. Three or four years later, the Miners acquired a mate for their bear. The bears lived together several years, but no cubs came from this union. (Information, Nell Sullivan; image, Frederick Smith.)

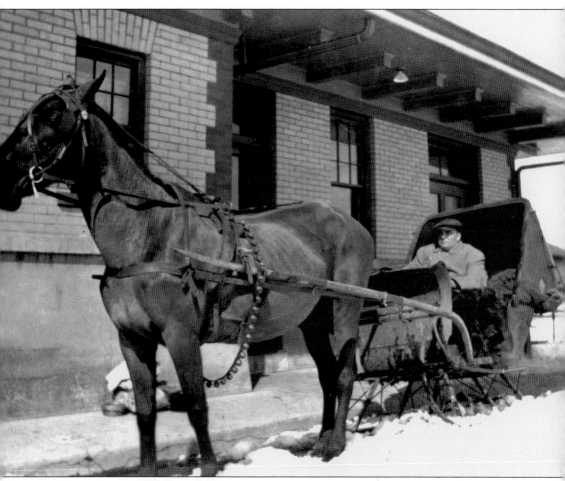

Pictured c. 1920 are George Laramie and his beautiful but timid mare, Pansy. One Sunday afternoon, Laramie took his pregnant wife, Clara, and four-year-old nephew, Roy Longtin, to visit his sister and brother-in-law, Julia and Benjamin Minckler, on the Bugby Road, about two miles away. It was was nearing dusk when they left to return home. On the way back, they met a big black bear ambling along the road. Horses are often afraid of bears, so Laramie had all he could do to hold Pansy on the road and get past the bear without tipping the carriage. The mare headed home as fast as possible. In the meantime, a pig named Porky had gotten out of the pen and gone into the carriage house, where it became tangled in an old coat. The pig, with its legs in the sleeves of the coat, came out to meet the carriage, which was entering the driveway. Pansy went wild again. Laramie had to get his wife and nephew out of the carriage and then somehow get Pansy into the stall. So, he drove Pansy to face the porch with her head over the railing and had his wife hold the reins until he could get out and hold Pansy's bridle. Then he took off his jacket, held it over Pansy's head, and led the mare into the stall. (Information, Marie Laramie Gennett.)

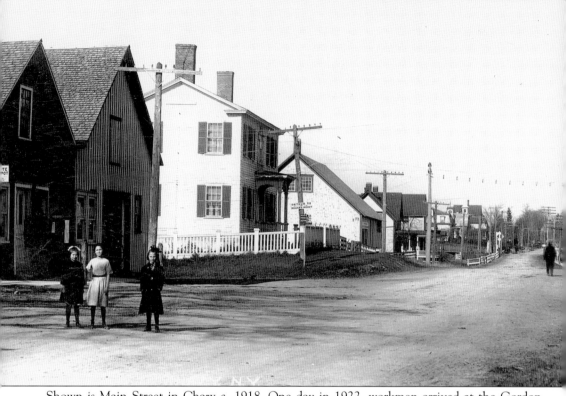

Shown is Main Street in Chazy *c.* 1918. One day in 1922, workmen arrived at the Gordon house, on Route 9 just south of Chazy village, to install electric wiring. Although the center of Chazy had been electrified about four years earlier, the Gordons had been using kerosene lamps. These lamps had a strong smell and coated their glass chimneys with soot. After the workmen left, the Gordons had one light hanging from the ceiling in each room, and the whole house was much brighter. (Information, Grace Gordon.)

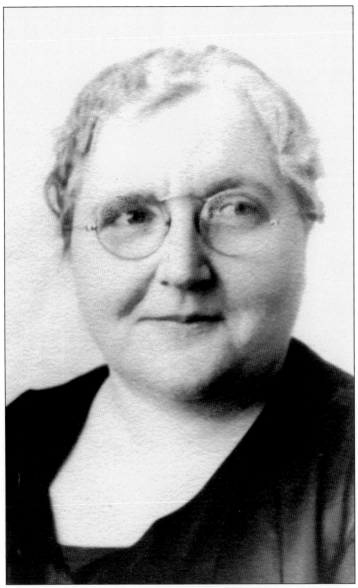

Shown is Harriet McDowell Clark. One Friday in 1926, the principal of the West Chazy School made a visit to Harriet Clark in Chazy village. The school was badly in need of a first-grade teacher, and Harriet Clark was a licensed teacher. She accepted the job offer and planned to start the next Monday. There was only one problem; she did not know how to drive. At that time, no test was required to get a driver's license. A few years earlier, she had purchased a license in Plattsburgh but had never used it. Now, she would need to drive to school every day. Over the weekend, therefore, her husband showed her how to start, stop, shift gears, back up, and so forth. Things went smoothly until she came up the hill over the railroad tracks in West Chazy. When she approached a traffic dummy in an intersection at the top of the hill, Fred Lougy walked across the road from Robinson's store. Lougy was about six feet six inches tall, and his presence so distracted her that she buzzed into the intersection, went around the dummy, and drove back down the hill. The traffic dummies were later removed because drivers kept bumping into them. (Information and image, George W. Clark.)

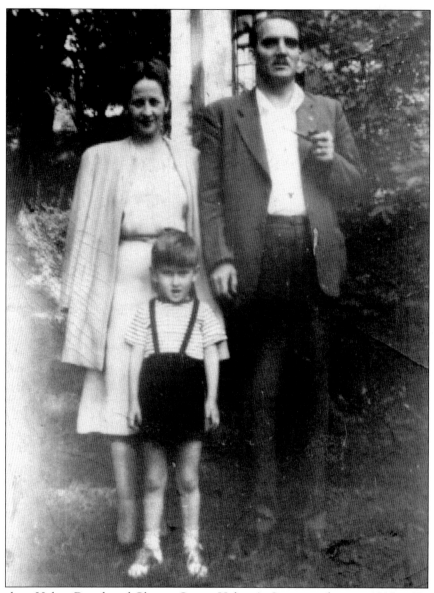

Pictured are Helen, David, and Clinton Sweet. Helen A. Sweet was born in 1905 at Hannibal, Missouri, and was one of the eight children of Fenton and Annette (Douglas) Morris. She went to Lindonwood College in St. Charles, Missouri. Her family moved to Lake Worth, Florida, where she met Clinton Wallace Sweet, whom she married in 1927. The Sweets were married in a little church at Del Ray Beach, Florida, and then moved to Chazy Landing. Clinton Sweet worked for his father, William Sweet, on the Twin Boys Ferry, along with his brother Gerald. Clinton Sweet earned his engineer's license and later took charge of advertising. The Sweets had three children: Clinton Wallace II, William Morris, and David McCord Sweet. For many years, the family moved to Florida after the ferry season closed in December and then back to Chazy to start the ferry in May. Helen Sweet adapted wisely to the northern winters by insisting that her father-in-law install the new door on their garage at the east side, where it would be plowed for the milk truck. The snowdrifts on the west side were formidable. (Image, Helen Sweet.)

GEORGE H. SAXE
GENERAL COUNTRY STORE
CHAZY, N. Y.

We give the best service possible
We endeavor to accommodate our customers
We handle the best that's put up in Groceries

A poem appears on the reverse of this George Saxe store advertisement. (Image, Kim Neverett Howley.)

The Wreck of the Julie Plante

On one dark night on Lac Champlain
  De win' she blow, blow, blow,
An' de crew of the wood scow "Julie Plante"
  Got scare an' run below.
For de win' she blow lak hurricane,
  Bimeby she blow some more,
An' de scow bus up on Lac Champlain
  Wan arpent from de shore.

De Captinne walk on de front deck,
  An' walk de hin' deck too,
He call de crew from up de hole,
  He call de cook also.
De cook she's name was Rosie,
  Was come from Montreal,
Was chambre maid on lumber barge
  On de Grande Lachine Canal.

De win' she blow from nor'-eas'-wes',
  De sout' win' she blow too,
W'en Rosie cry "Mon Cher Captinne
  Mon Cher, w'at shall I do?"
Den de Captinne trow de big ankerre,
  But still de scow she dreef,
De crew he can't pass on de shore,
  Becos' he los' hees skeef.

De night was dark lak' one black cat,
  De wave run high and fas',
W'en de Captinne tak' de Rosie girl
  An' tie her to de mas',
Den he also take de life preserve
  An jomb off on de lak',
An' say "Good-bye, ma Rosie dear,
  I go drown for your sak'."

Nex' morning very early,
  'Bout haf' pas' two-t'ree-four—
De Captinne—scow—an' de poor Rosie
  Was corpses on de shore.
"For de win' she blow lak' hurricane,
  Bimeby she blow some more,
An' de scow bus' up on Lac Champlain
Wan arpent from de shore."

MORAL:

Now all good wood scow sailor man
  Tak' warning by dat storm
An' go an' marry some nice French girl
  An' leev on one beeg farm.
De win' can blow lake hurricane,
  An' spose she blow some more,
You can't get drown on Lac Champlain
  So long you stay on shore.

The Wreck of the Julie Plante was done by D.T. Trombly. Known as "Batiste," Trombly would hand this out on the Twin Boys Ferry. (Image, Kim Neverett Howley.)

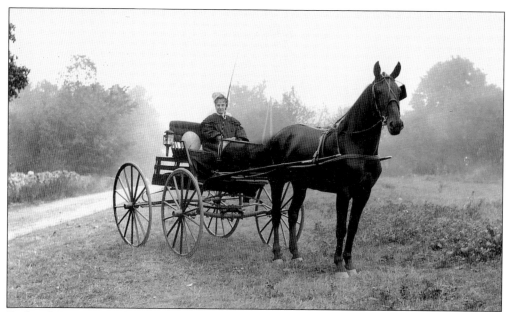

Frederick B. Townsend, whose wife is shown in this *c*. 1913 photograph, was the designer for Chazy Central Rural School.

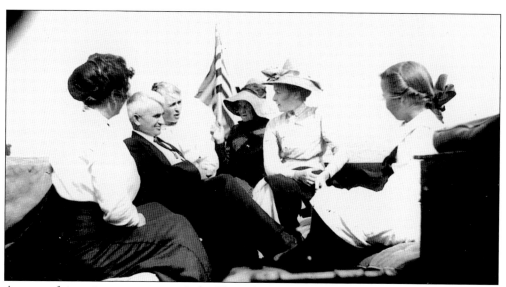

A group of six enjoys an outing on Lake Champlain *c*. 1920. (Image, Matt Clark.)

Deborah Harris, shown here with a catch of northern pike, was a Quaker. (Image, David Martin.)

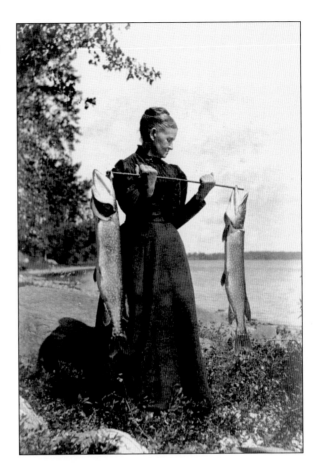

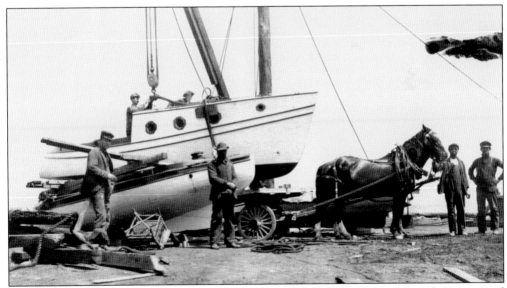

The boat shown in this 1906 image was owned by Will Robinson, David Harris, and Herb Attwood. The men seen here are unidentified. (Image, David Martin.)

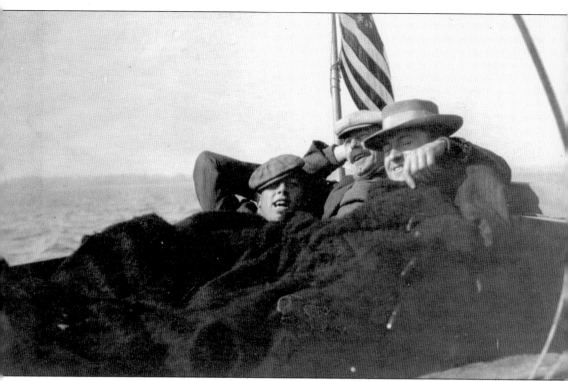

In this boat are, from left to right, Fred Carnes, Will Robinson, and an unidentified boy. (Image, David Martin.)

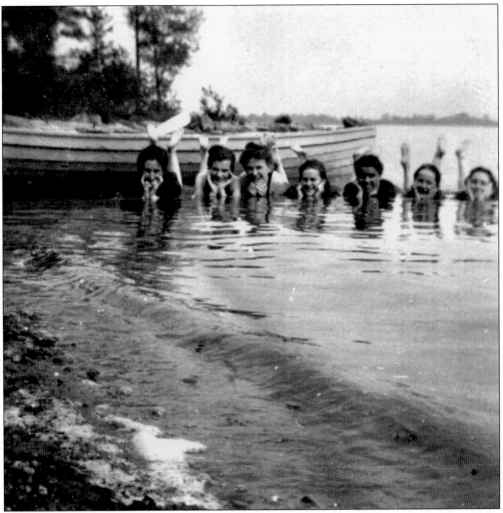

This 1912 photograph shows Florence Doane (left) and her friends cooling off in Lake Champlain. (Image, Helen Saxe Booth.)

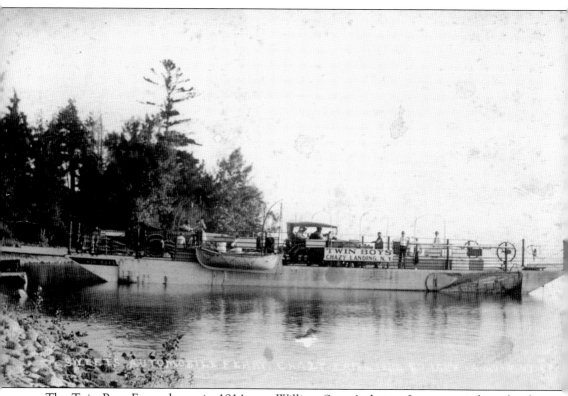

The Twin Boys Ferry, shown in 1914, was William Sweet's design. It was carried out by the Champlain boatyard. The ferry kept all of the best of the old design with several new innovations, such as the four leeboards. Captain Seely, the steamboat inspector from Washington, D.C., came to inspect and stayed to admire the ferry. Gerald Sweet remembers Captain Seely saying, "Will, I don't know how you did it but it is the best . . . designed ferry for the lake or a river I've ever seen. When you dock and let down her leeboards, she is like a cow with four legs stuck in the mud. You can't move her." Seely sent other boatbuilders and ferry owners to study the ferry from as far west as the Mississippi River. (Image, Helen Saxe Booth.)

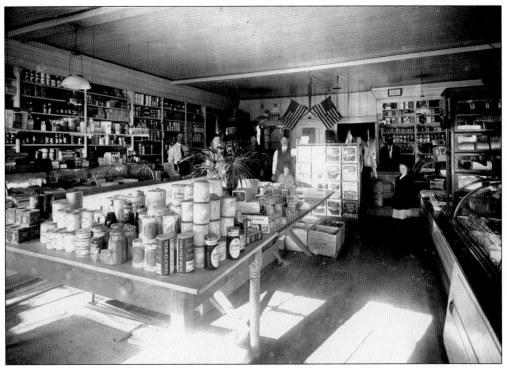

Pictured is George Saxe's store, in Chazy. (Image, Jane Hess.)

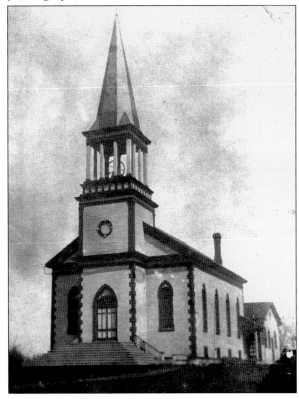

The Presbyterian Church of Chazy
is seen here. (Image, Jane Hess.)

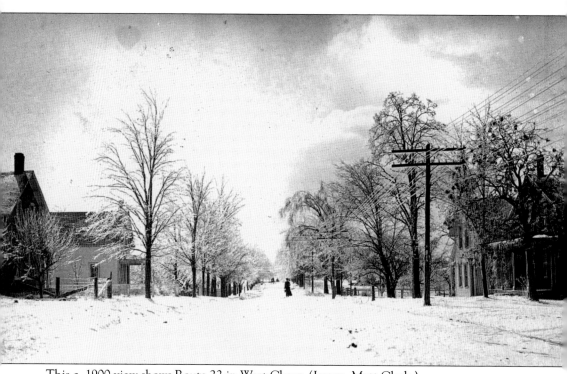

This *c.* 1900 view shows Route 22 in West Chazy. (Image, Matt Clark.)

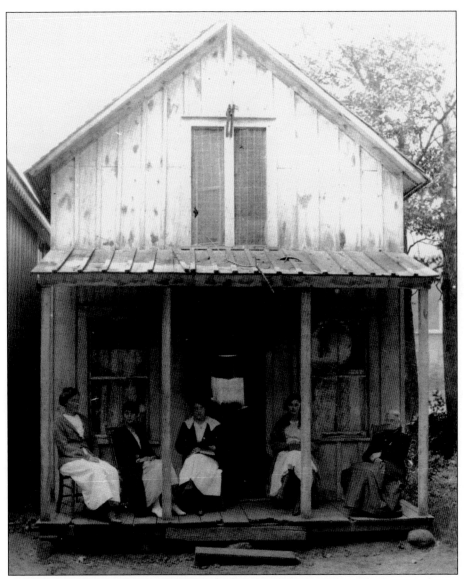

Pictured in 1920 is the Amasa Spellman house, located in Sciota. Chazy sat right on the rumrunning route from Canada into the United States. Sometimes, a bootlegger would hide his car in the area if it broke down. Hershey Trombly got a phone call one night from some bootleggers saying they had hidden their car behind his barn. They offered him a bottle of liquor for hiding his car, and he drank some of it the next day. Later that same day, he had to go to school to take a high school entrance exam. He passed and became the first Trombly to graduate from Chazy Central Rural School. The bootleggers soon came back, fixed the car, and went on their way. One evening, when the Trombly family was sitting at the supper table, the kitchen door slammed open and a man said, "Where can I hide?" Right behind him was officer Hamilton McRae of the boarder patrol. The man took one look and jumped right through the *closed* kitchen window. His neck got caught in the clothesline across the porch. He got up and ran across the road into Bill Bechard's yard and right into another clothesline. That is where McRae caught up with him. When he got out of jail, the man came back and paid the Tromblys for the window. (Information, Lyles Trombly.)

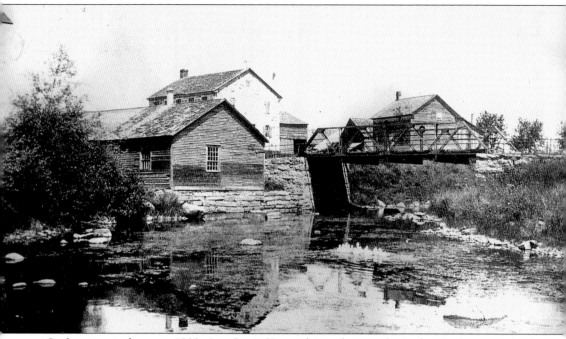

Suckortown is shown *c.* 1880. Ann Lucia Yanowski was born and raised in Suckortown. In the spring, when the dam was opened, she and her neighbors would gather to catch fish to sell or to eat. They would also jump off the dikes into the river at the bottom of the dam, which served as the neighborhood pool. One end was about two feet deep with a cement bottom. During the summer, Yanowski and her friends helped grow and sell crops, including strawberries, blueberries, long blackberries, and short blackberries. They chased the farm animals and gathered eggs in the barns. To get to school, they took a horse-drawn bus, with heated bricks to keep their feet warm. In the winter, they skated on the river, sledded down the hills, and made snow tunnels (some of which ran from the barn to the house). At maple sugar time, they would tap the trees, gather the sap, and make syrup. (Information, Ann Lucia Yanowski.)

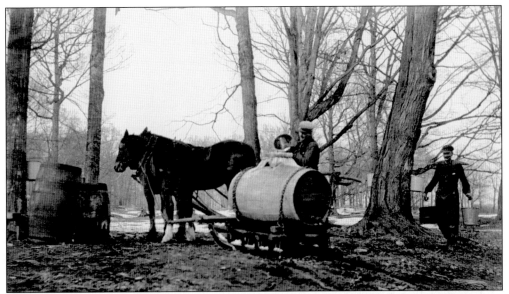

This photograph shows the gathering of sap to make maple syrup. (Image, David Martin.)

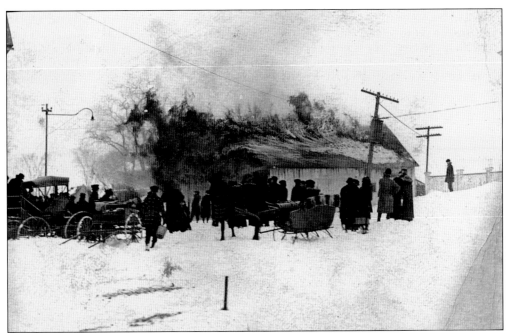

John W. Talford's store, located on Main Street, burned in 1920. After the fire, Talford continued the business in the barn. Eventually, the barn also burned. In this view, Stanley North is the man in the plaid coat.

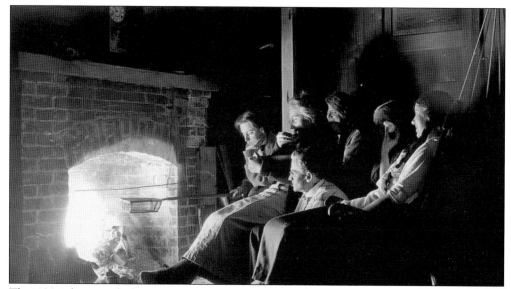

This 1914 photograph shows a group popping corn. (Image, Matt Clark.)

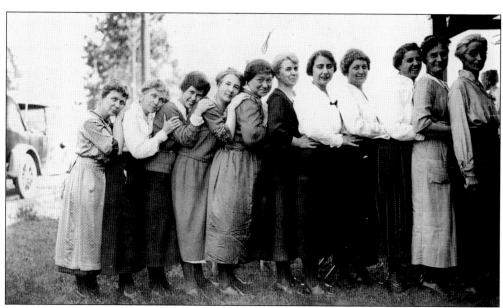

West Chazy women are shown in this 1915 photograph. (Image, Matt Clark.)

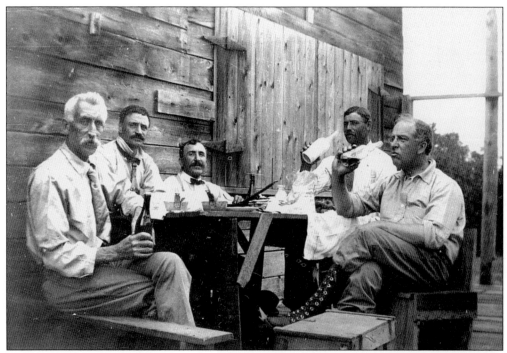

Five men relax in West Chazy in 1910. From left to right are Freehold Sheldon, two unidentified men, William Atwood, and ? Swift (a doctor).

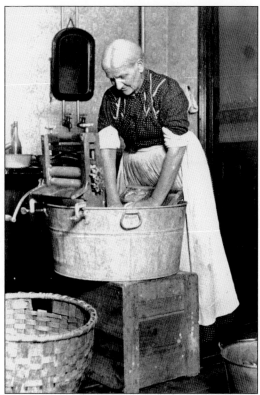

Seen here is Fanny Brothers during an early-20-century washday. (Image, David Martin.)

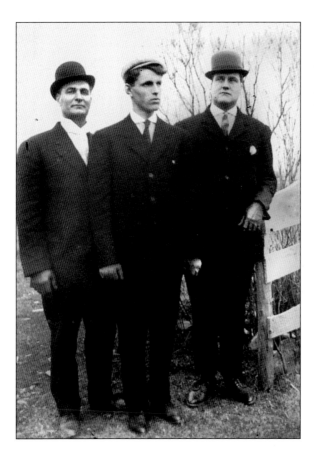

Each of these well-dressed men, from left to right, Alex Ferryall, Stanley A. North, and George W. Clark, is gazing in a different direction. The photograph was taken in 1908 in Chazy.

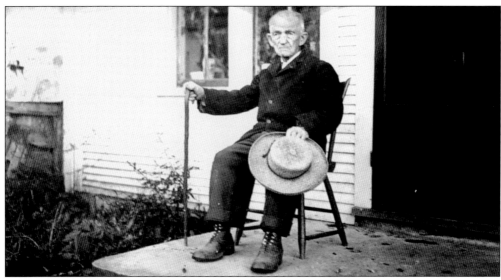

Robert Scott McCullough takes a break on his porch in October 1920.

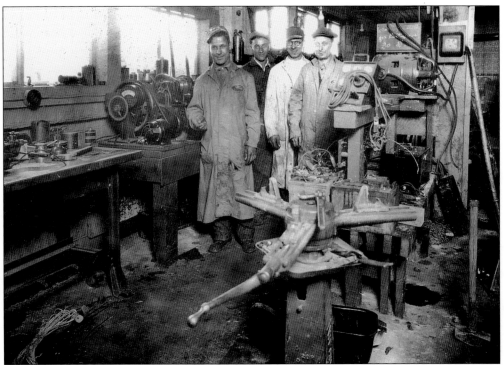

With smiles, from left to right, Austin Brunelle, Peter Patenaude, Frank Brunelle, and Hubert Patenaude pause for a picture *c*. 1928. The Patenaudes operated a garage in Chazy and serviced automobiles. The garage was located where the Ford dealership is today.

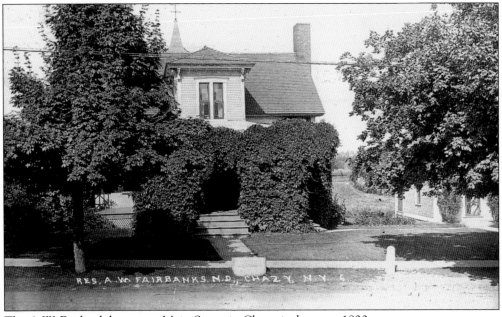

RES. A. W. FAIRBANKS, N.D., CHAZY, N.Y. 6

The A.W. Fairbank house, on Main Street in Chazy, is shown *c*. 1920.

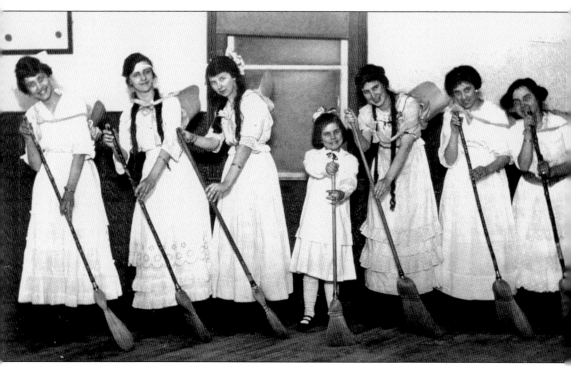

These young women from West Chazy are shown sweeping in 1916. From left to right are Addie Goodale, Marion Rae, Ila Alison, Merris Robinson, Vera Robinson, Marion Goodale, and Ethle LaPier. (Image, David Martin.)

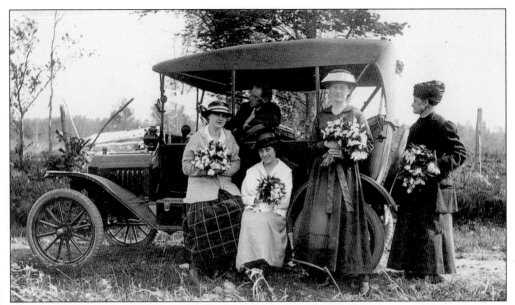

Pictured here with friends, Doris Hunsinger and Marion Goodale have discovered a new way to travel. (Image, Matt Clark.)

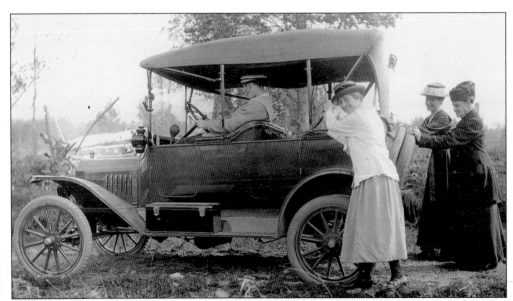

Stuff can happen on the road, as seen in this photograph. Doris Hunsinger is pictured driving the vehicle, and Marion Goodale is shown in the white blouse. (Image, Matt Clark.)

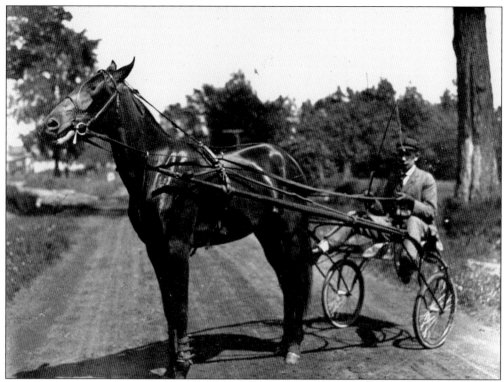

Pictured is Orin Minkler, of the Minkler Road.

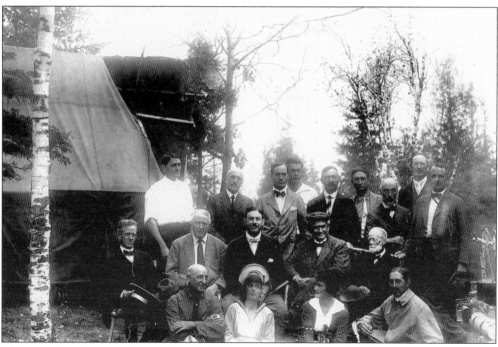

This camping photograph was taken in 1910.

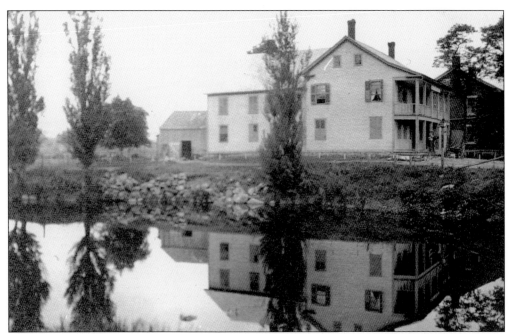

The Collins Hotel, located on Main Street along the Chazy River, is pictured here.

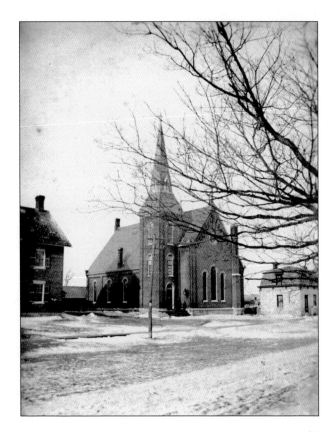

This view shows the Methodist church in Chazy village. (Image, Jane Hess.)

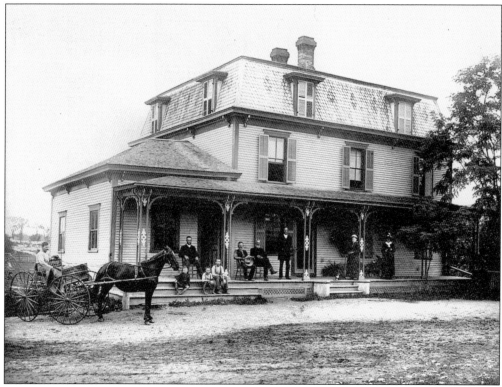

The Red Lion Hotel opened in 1835. It was sold to John McCullough in 1864 and became known as the McCullough Hotel. In the early 1900s, it was discontinued as a hotel, and eventually, it was torn down. It was located at the intersection of Main Street and the Fisk Road.

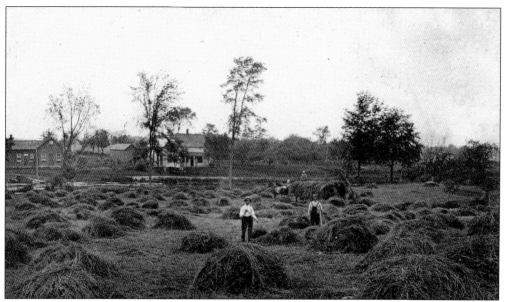

J.F. Gilbert's hayfield is shown in a view looking west. The house is on River Street in Chazy.

Shown in this view of the Saxe family are, from left to right, the following: (front row) Arthur Saxe, Elizabeth Saxe, and Lizzie Merrihew; (back row) George and Lottie Saxe. (Image, Jane Hess.)

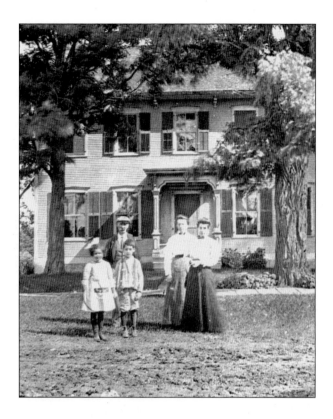

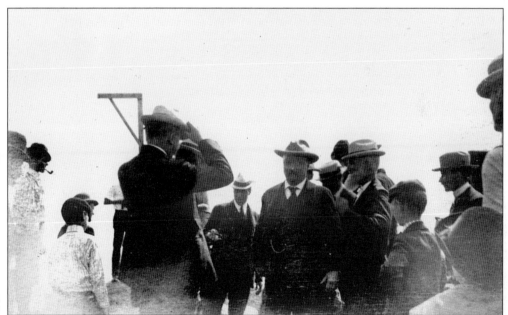

Vice Pres. Theodore Roosevelt was welcomed at Fisk's Landing on Isle La Motte, Vermont, on September 6, 1901. Admirers from Chazy were on hand, and one snapped this photograph. On the same day in Buffalo, Pres. William McKinley was shot, and he succumbed to his wounds a week later, making Roosevelt the president. (Image, David Martin.)

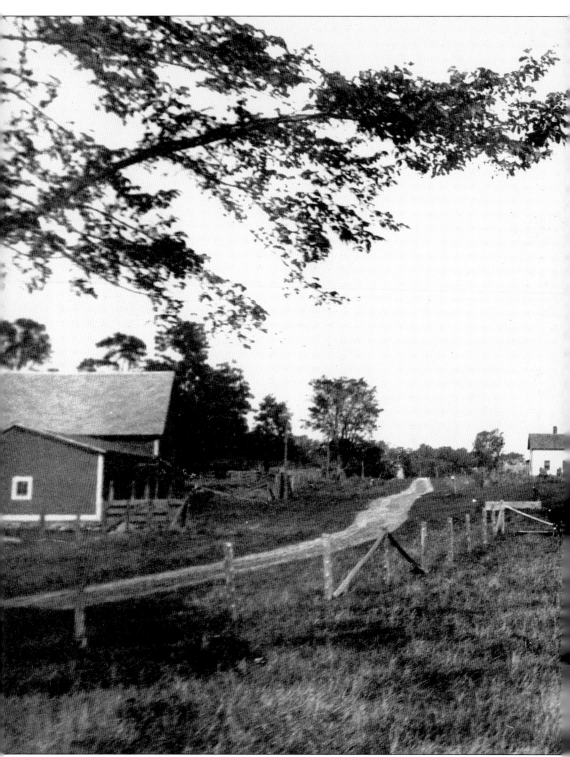

The Louis Trombly farm, located on the Lake Shore Road, is shown c. 1910. Over the years, the farm was also owned by Henry Oliver, Walter Clukey, and

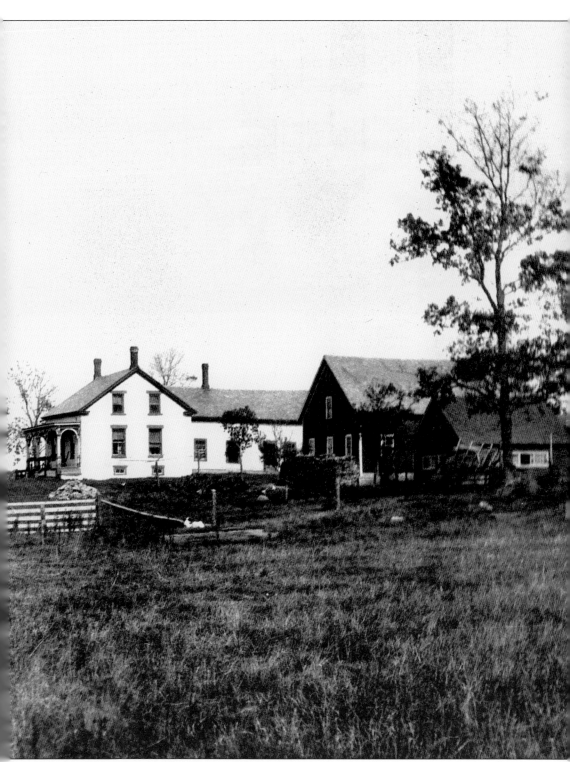

Richard Clukey. Giroux's Poultry owns it today.

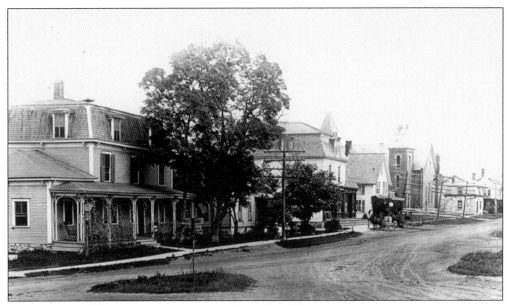

Main Street in Chazy is shown as it appeared in 1910. This view looks north.

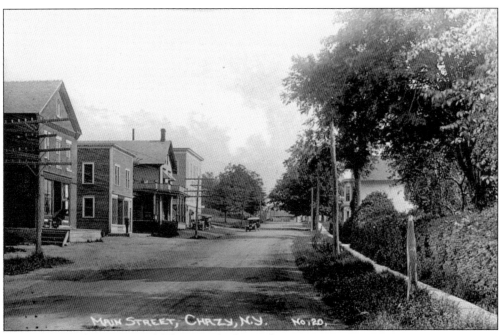

Main Street is shown in 1915. This view looks south.

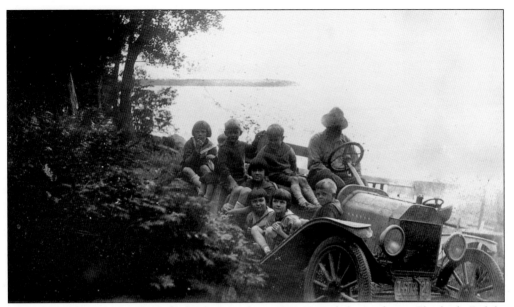

Louis Trombly gives the Hubbell children a ride in 1929. From left to right are Elizabeth, Ralph, John, an unidentified person, Sophie, Dorothy, and George Hubbell.

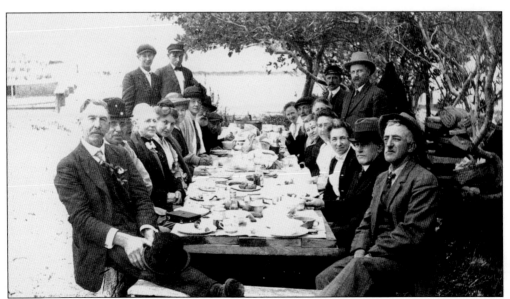

Dressed in fine clothes, these people enjoy a picnic on the shore of Lake Champlain. (Image, David Martin.)

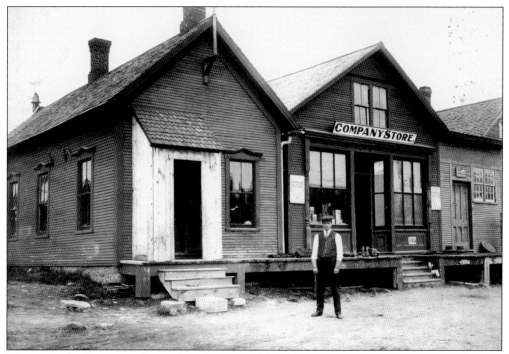

Warren Fairbank poses in front of the Chazy Marble and Lime store on Route 9 just south of the orchard. (Image, Helen Saxe Booth.)

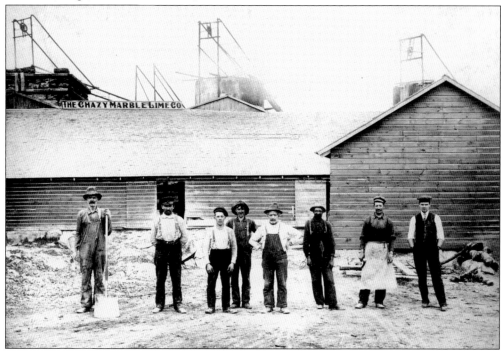

This photograph was taken at the Chazy Marble and Lime Company in 1905. From left to right are John Bolia, Napoleon Abare, Simeon Wells, an unidentified person, Peter Wells, Frank Donah, Pete Mosse, and Warren Fairbank. (Image, Helen Saxe Booth.)

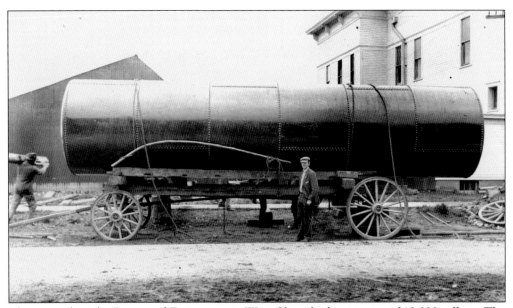

The gas tank at the Brean and Deno store in West Chazy had a capacity of 10,000 gallons. The hole for the tank had to be hand dug. (Image, David Martin.)

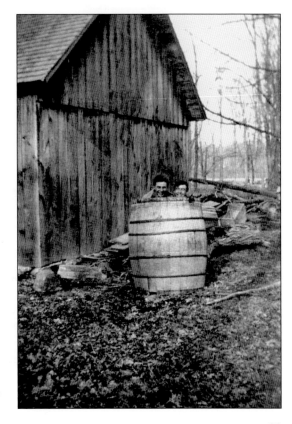

This photograph shows West Chazy men in a rain barrel. (Image, David Martin.)

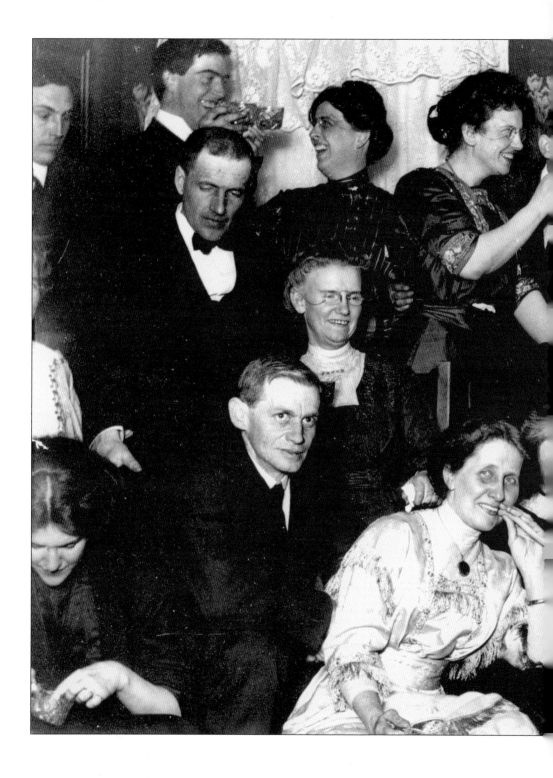

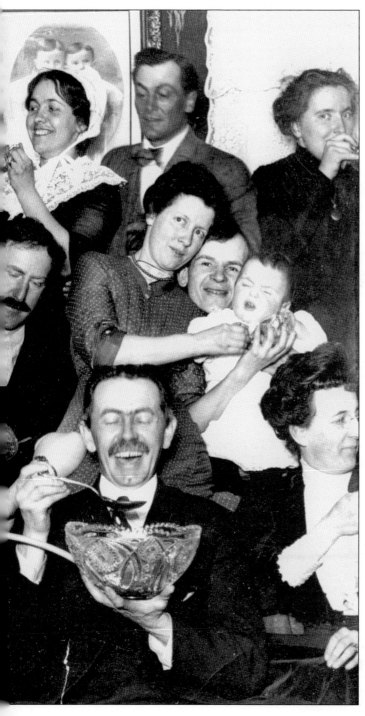

This party was held in West Chazy on March 13, 1912. From left to right are the following: (front row) Bessie Lucia, David Harris, Celia Dustin, Mattie Stiles, William H. Robinson, and Cora Clark; (middle row) Emma Carlton, Matt Clark, Mary Foster, Sherman Foster, and Grace Foster (baby); (back row) Henry Fuller, Fred Carnes (with cups), Rev. Frank Terrell, ? French, Helen Robinson, Harry Stiles, Blanche Terrell, Miller Dustin, and Harriet McDowell. (Image, David Martin.)

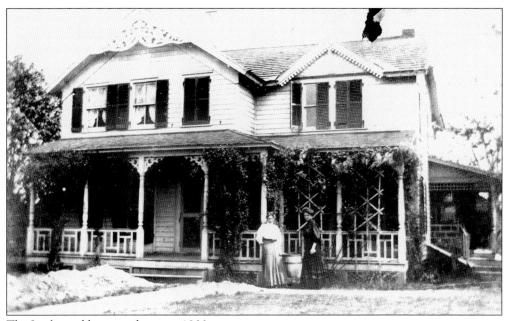

The Lockwood house is shown *c*. 1900.

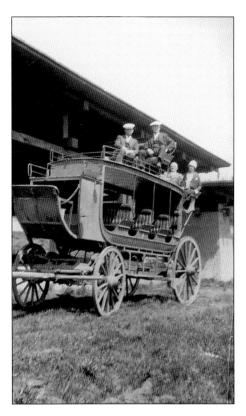

A stagecoach is pictured in this 1920 view. (Image, C.D. Miller.)

Three

1930–1939

Despite the tough times of the 1930s, mention of the Great Depression rarely appears when Chazyites reminisce about their childhood. Perhaps this is because Chazy is largely rural and farms breed self-reliant people.

Martin Hewson grew up in the Depression years and recalls many people who were having a hard time, as work was scarce and the pay was low. On the farm, however, life was much easier. Hewson's father would give a neighbor who was out of work a turkey, beans, vegetables, and firewood. The family raised chickens, turkeys, pigs, and cows and therefore had its own bacon, ham, eggs, milk, butter, vegetables, flour, apples, and meats. Hewson's mother always had a large vegetable garden and fruits that she canned for the winter months. Salting preserved some of the meats and vegetables. There was also a small apple orchard, and in the fall the Hewsons would take the apples to a nearby pressing mill for processing into cider and vinegar for the winter.

For a number of years, the Hewsons had a hired hand, who lived with his wife and five children in a tenant house at the end of the farm. The man received his rent free, a large plowed piece of land for a garden, firewood, milk, eggs, and $1 per day for a five-day week from morning to night. He would help with the milking chores, tending to the care of the cows, haying, and harvesting.

For fuel, the Hewsons went into their woods and cut wood to be used in the kitchen stove and, during the winter months, in the furnace (along with coal).

Later, during the rationing of World War II, farmers were able to get gasoline and tires. Because farmers had their food, rationing was not an issue. Farm families were truly fortunate.

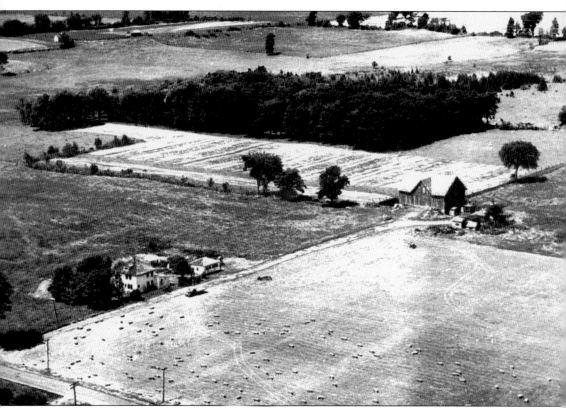

This scene shows the Hewson Farm in Chazy. When the corn was growing, young Martin Hewson would rise early, hitch up the team of horses to the two-horse cultivator, and ride for several hours, steering the harrows, with his feet digging up the dirt and weeds in the many rows of field corn. He would do this for weeks until the corn got too high. (Image, Martin Hewson.)

Pictured are Sue Norton Bruce and her brother Bud in front of Sunnyside Cottage. Sue Bruce was born Marguerite E. Norton in Port Henry on November 22, 1920, to Homer J. and Sarah Ellen (Kimball) Norton. Early on, her sister started calling her Sue. Homer Norton was an engineer working on the railroad in Port Henry. In 1927, the foreman, a Mr. Evans, offered Norton a job at the Chazy Lime Kiln, operating a large crane. Norton came to town ahead of his family and stayed with the Garfield brothers, who took in boarders. Sarah Norton and the children—Esther, Bud, and Sue—also stayed at the Garfields' for a while until they moved to Sunnyside Cottage down the street. The railroad tracks ran behind the house. Every time the children heard their father blow the whistle to announce that he was coming with the crane up the main tracks, they would run through the fields to catch a ride with him. (Information and image, Sue Norton Bruce.)

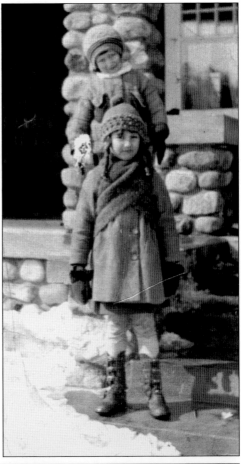

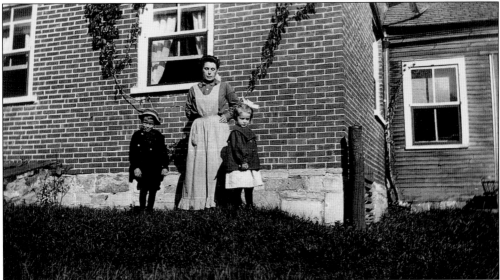

Members of the Hay family stand outside their home in West Chazy. From left to right are William Hay, Emma Corbin Hay, and Eleanor Hay.

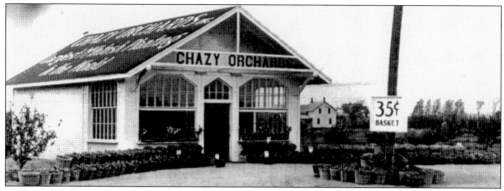

Shown is the Chazy Orchard store. The Rasmussen family came from Champaign, Illinois, by train to Chazy in 1932. George Rasmussen got a job at the orchard as a beekeeper, and the family lived in an orchard house by the lake. After a year, Rasmussen's job changed and the family moved across the yard to a house with a backyard tree with a swing in it and a brook running beside the house to the lake. Rasmussen had to care for the greenhouse and help at the open-air market on Route 9, selling apples, honey, flowers, melons, and other vegetables. In the winter, when work was hard to find, he used his own pickup truck to sell apples door-to-door. His wife made clothes from old shirts and dresses for their two daughters, Ann and Alice Lou. She once made Alice Lou a beautiful coat out of a red blanket. (Information and image, Alice Lou Sanger.)

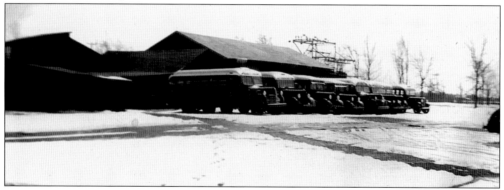

Chazy school buses of the 1940s are shown. Recently, a school assignment from May 20, 1932, was discovered under a bus seat. The bus was one of William H. Miner's buses, now housed in a museum at the Miner Farm. Aline Bechard Terry, who found the paper, happens to be a cousin of Gabrielle Bechard, who did the assignment as a fourth- or fifth-grader.

"When I was a little girl in the colonial days we had very few toys. Those that we had were made out of wood. But we knew many games like hop scotch, puss in corner, blind man's bluff, and many different kinds of tag.

"There was much work for us to do on the farms. We had to bring in wood for the fireplace and feed the livestock. The girls had to cook the food and keep the room clean. We couldn't play before our work was done. We had to be very obedient.

"The daughters of the rich had some work to do too. They embroidered stitches and practiced standing correctly and many things of etiquette.

"There were many sports we could do also. Like horse racing, boat racing, swimming, and foot racing. We enjoyed those as much as the boys did.

"I wonder if in two hundred years from now the amusement we enjoyed will be enjoyed in the same way?"

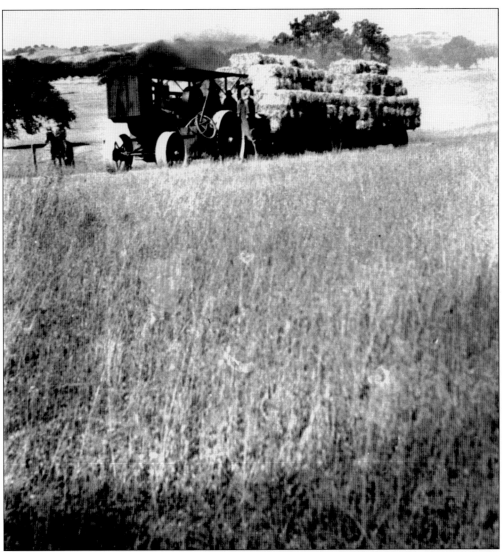

Men work in the fields at the Miner Farm *c.* 1930. Frederick Parrot worked on the farm for many years. Every night after supper, he would go to the pastures to check on the cows. Daughter Marion Parrot and her friend Sally Martin would visit him at the farm and get into mischief. They would ride their bicycles through the horse barn, hitting the stalls with sticks and making the horses rear up and neigh. The farm finally got electric milking machines, but Parrott still tended to each cow, making sure the milk was pasteurized and separated properly. One year, he set a record by milking one cow four times a day and producing the most milk with the highest fat content. After that, he crossed one of his Black Angus with a buffalo and created Beefalo meat. (Information, Marion Parrot Runge.)

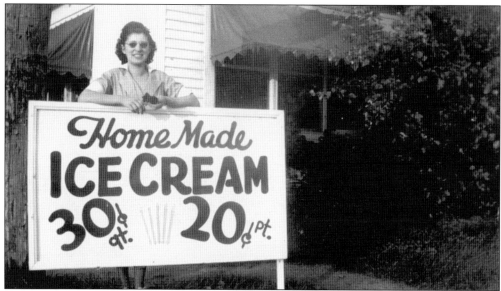

Alice Guay is shown at Bay View Cabins, on Route 9. Making ice cream was a favorite event at the Laramie farm. The family had its own eggs and cream and also had a carriage steppingstone near the back porch—the perfect place to make ice cream. Clara Laramie would make a delicious pudding. Her husband, George, would use a hammer to break up ice in a burlap bag. He would then put the pudding and cream into the canister. The dasher would go in, and the cover would go on. George would carefully place the ice with salt around the canister and begin turning the handle on the side. Eventually, the ice cream froze. Sometimes, strawberries, walnuts, or pineapple would be added. Licking the dasher was the best part of all. (Information, Marie Laramie Gennett; image, Rita Trombly.)

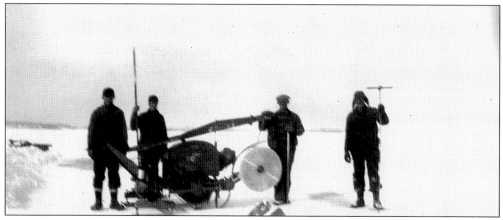

Workers cut ice on Lake Champlain. In 1931, Louis B. Jubert started a meat business at his dairy farm in Sciota. Jubert constructed a small building on his property to house a cooler and a meat department. He then established a successful meat route that served the village of Chazy as well as Sciota. The meat was cooled with ice that cost 3¢ a block. Jubert would store up to 1,000 blocks encased in sawdust to carry him through the summer and fall. He once adapted the wringer from his wife's gas-operated Maytag washer to use as a meat grinder. The farm got electricity in 1941, and a meat grinder was one of his first purchases. In 1942, Jubert gave up the meat business after it became difficult to get meat during wartime rationing. (Information, Harold and Barbara Jubert.)

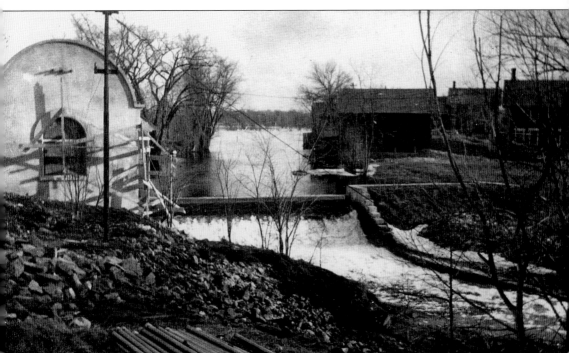

Shown is the Miner powerhouse on the Chazy River in the village. Armand Duprey was born in 1930 in the house that is by the river in back of what used to be McCuen's Store. His two older brothers, George and Russell, would go to the store and get some large pieces of cardboard so they could slide down the hill behind the barbershop to the river. It was a good place to go sledding but was dangerous for its proximity to the water. One day, the boys' father solved this problem by throwing their sled into the river. In 1933, the Dupreys moved to the Duprey Road house, where there were barns and 20 acres of land. Armand Duprey used to play cowboy on horses with Jim Blair. He used leather and other materials to make regular shoes look like cowboy boots. He once made a saddle from barrel staves and sheepskin. He hid the saddle from his father over some boards on the ceiling of the barn. The saddle, however, came down one day and hit Armand Duprey in the mouth, breaking a front tooth. After a few days, the sore tooth had to be pulled by the local dentist, Dr. Orville Narreau. (Information, Bob Cheeseman.)

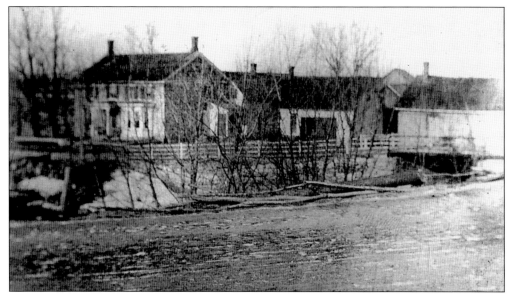

Pictured here is the Solomon Fisk home, located on the Fisk Road along the Chazy River in Chazy.

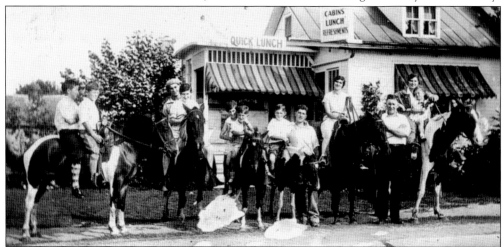

Shown here are the Bay View Cabins. Members of the Guay family, from left to right, are Ferdinand "Willie", Phillip, Maurice "Hank", Olive, Rita, Paul, Arthur, Van, Alma, Valmore, Alice, and Anita Guay. In 1926, when seven-year-old Rita started first grade, she and several of her siblings rode the horse-drawn wagon bus for the three-mile trip to Chazy Central Rural School. She faced the same challenge as did many students who came from homes where only French was spoken: the inability to speak English made the transition to school difficult. Doing well at school was only half of her parents' expectation; helping out at home was equally valued. Her father, Valmore Guay, owned a dairy farm with a herd of 20 cows. The farm was situated between Route 9 on the west and Lake Champlain on the east. All of the children, according to their abilities, played their role in helping the family make ends meet. Eldest sons, Arthur and Maurice, milked the cows and did related farm chores. Phillip and Ferdinand cleaned and maintained the tourist cabins, and Ferdinand also washed dishes. Alice and Rita served as waitresses in the Bay View Restaurant, and Olive had household chores and took tourists for scenic horseback rides through the pastures to the lake. (Information and image, Rita Guay Trombly.)

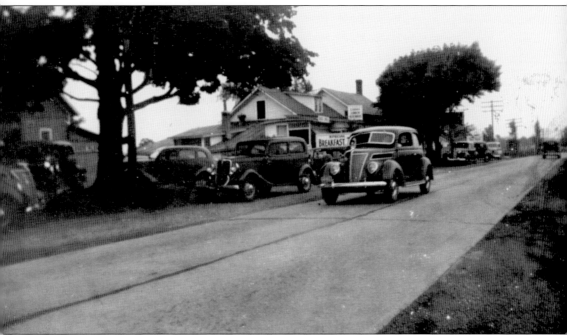

During the years from 1930 to 1935, Sundays were special days for Rita Guay at the Bay View Restaurant. Cars would line both sides of Route 9 when families came to enjoy a home-cooked meal for an affordable price. For 50¢, the Sunday lunch consisted of a half of a broiler chicken, choice of potatoes, a garden-grown vegetable, homemade bread and butter, coffee, homemade pie, and hand-churned ice cream. Rita's mother, Alma Corbierre Guay, had a reputation for her cooking, and Rita's future mother-in-law, Martha Mousseau Trombly, extended that reputation with her delicious homemade pies. After lunch, families would relax on the wooden gliders and catch up on the news of the community. The clientele was largely local but included the tourists who stayed at the family's Bay View Cabins, which offered running water, flush toilets, and (for some) heat. A take-out window offered ice cream and cigarettes. The hand churner was eventually replaced by an electric ice-cream machine. Except on Sundays, sandwiches could be bought at the takeout window, normally served by Rita and Anita Guay. (Information and image, Rita Guay Trombly.)

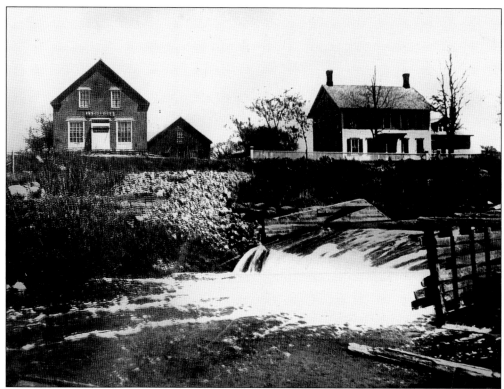

Shown is the Merrihew store, located just south of the museum in Chazy.

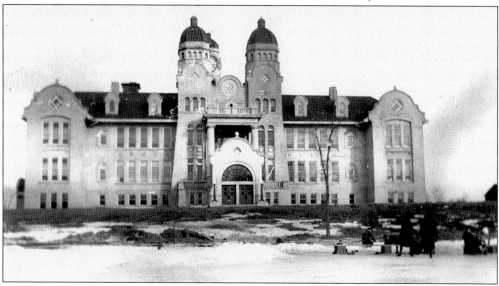

Shown is the Chazy Central Rural School. Louisa B. Inglas, the school principal, was nicknamed "Bulldog." One day, Lyles Trombly and Red Oliver were at their lockers when they saw a small dog wandering in the hall. There was an elevator with open doors right there, so they put the dog into it. The doors immediately closed, and the elevator went up. They ran up the stairs to beat the elevator. Then, they saw the principal with her key in the elevator, opening it. Out ran the dog, and away ran the two boys. (Information, Lyles Trombly.)

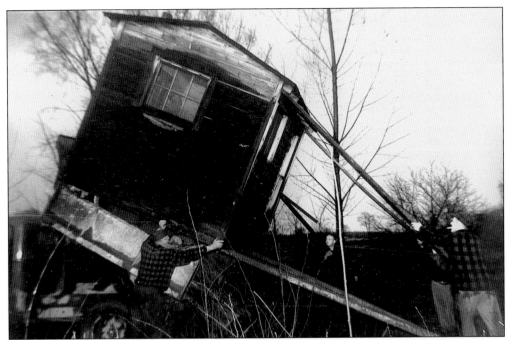

The train station in Sciota is shown in this 1930s view. The station was moved to Cooperville to replace one that had burned. The line that went through Sciota was shut down in 1925.

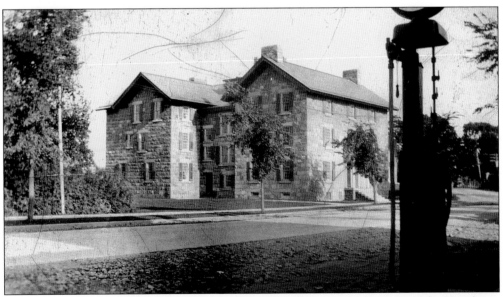

Pictured is the Alice T. Miner Museum. Benjamin Wait, Ebenezer Ascher Scott, John Haughran, Napoleon Trombly, Lafayette F. Merrihew, John H. McCuen, Henry Buckman, Fletcher Gilbert, J. Philander Forbes, and C.H. Jones all owned and operated businesses from this location. In the early 1900s, William H. Miner purchased the property and converted it into a museum. (Information, Nell B. Sullivan and David K. Martin.)

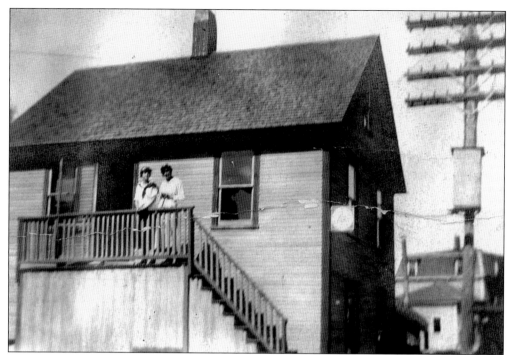

The Chazy telephone company was started in 1903. The telephone office was located at the intersection of the Fisk Road and Main Street. The building was torn down in the 1970s.

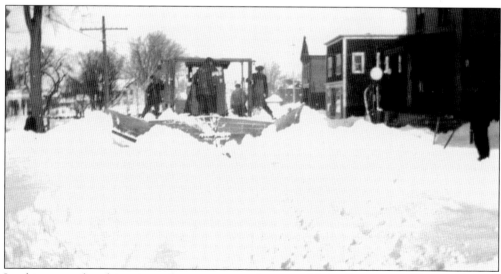

Looking north, this view shows a snowplow on Main Street in Chazy. (Image, Helen Saxe Booth.)

Four

1940–1959

As a student at Chazy Central Rural School, Marie Laramie Gennett was enrolled in the home economics class, and her job was to make sure the red bench cushion in her senior homeroom, the Shakespeare Room, was always neat and perfect. One day, she was mending the cushion with a needle and thread. She was sitting on the floor when a boy she knew walked in and sat down with his legs on either side of the cushion. While they talked, she inadvertently sewed the right leg of the boy's pants to the pillow. They found this little accident funny until they heard the familiar jingle of the principal's keys coming down the hall. The principal, Louisa B. Inglas, carried a key to every door in Clinton County. She was a strict woman and wore small glasses down on the bridge of her nose. It was the custom to stand and say hello when she entered the room. So, when she walked in, Marie Laramie and the boy stood up, pillow and all. When Inglas saw the pillow, she said, "I think there has been a sewing mishap." Marie claimed responsibility for the accident, but the principal punished them both by making them stay after school.

When Richard West attended Chazy Central between 1941 and 1954, there were green school buses with gold lettering outlined in red. He had the same first-grade teacher, Mrs. Robinson, as his father had had. His fourth-grade teacher was Helen Brown, who he says liked him so much that she kept him for two years. The school had two gyms and two swimming pools, but both pools were closed. During his high school years, he played two intramural sports (basketball and baseball) and received the Babe Ruth Sportsmanship Award. Truant officer John Beekman would patrol the high school lunchroom and would visit the student's home if he discovered an absence. After school, Richard West would rush to get his chores done so he could go in the living room and listen to radio shows that would last 15 minutes each. His favorite shows were *Batman and Robin*, *The Green Hornet*, *Sam Spade*, *The Fatman*, and *Sky King*.

Dorothy Parrot recalls that her whole family would gather in the sugar shacks for days at a time while her father boiled the sap. They would cook all their meals in the shack. They used the sugar and syrup from the sap in many of their meals. They used to boil their eggs in the boiling sap so the eggs would taste sweet. They made sugar cakes, sugar candies, and a granulated sugar from the sap. Dorothy Parrot married James LaDue in 1933. LaDue, who was from a family of men who died young, traveled alone by train to Montreal to seek the help of a man named Antoine Tetreault, believed to have healing powers because he was born the seventh son of a seventh son. The lifelines on the healer's palm formed a perfect heart. As the man passed his hands over LaDue's head toward his chest and down to his feet, LaDue could feel the heat move from those hands through him. The healer told him to go home and continue working for the railroad. LaDue did. He lived to have four sons and died at the age of 86 in 1999.

—Kristen Henry, Rebecca Beeman, and Cornelius Van Splinter

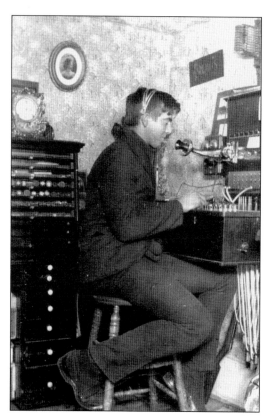

Fred Carnes served as the telephone operator in West Chazy. Years ago, the telephone system worked by transmitting "shorts" and "longs" by turning a crank. When you heard that, you knew you had a call. In the village of Chazy, on the second floor of what was Dumars', an operator handled special calls and any problems. Her switchboard looked out on Main Street toward the store across the street. Mrs. George L. Hubbell, known as "Gramma," would send her two daughters, Margie and Betty, to the store to do the family shopping. If she forgot to put an item on the list, she would ring the operator: "Do you see Margie and Betty at the store?" If the answer was yes, Gramma would ask the operator to call out to the girls to get whatever she had forgotten. (Information, Pete Hubbell; image, David Martin.)

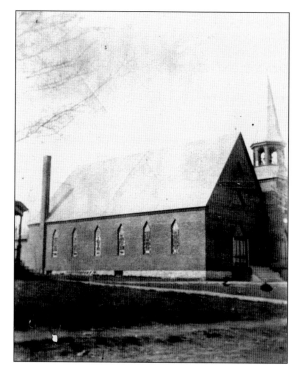

This is a view of the Catholic church. The Jensen family lived next to the church, which was only one block from the school. Still, the eldest daughter was always late for school. So, one morning she got to school and the principal met her at the door. To her surprise, the principal handed her an alarm clock. (Information, Jeb Bell; image, Jane Hess.)

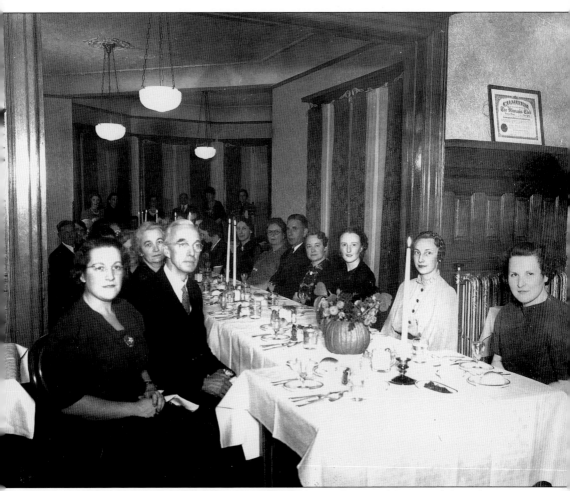

Teachers at Chazy Central Rural School are pictured at a dining table. seated from front to back are the following: (left) Dorothy LaBombard, John Beekman, Florence Beekman, and unidentified; (right) Syble Brown, two unidentified women, Helen Brown, and unidentified. When the Martins came to Chazy to teach in 1958, Gray Gables was in full swing as "the Teacherage." Living quarters for teachers were distributed in a curious manner. If you were a married male teacher, as David Martin was, you were given a spacious apartment rent free. If you were an unmarried female teacher, you were given room and board in the front part of Gray Gables. Married women teachers, however, were given no consideration, as it was felt their husbands would look out for them. Unmarried men teachers were expected to look after themselves. At that time, the school policy prohibited the school from hiring both a husband and a wife at the same time. It had to be one or the other. Garage space in the Methodist church shed next door rented for $8 a year. (Information, David Martin; image, Joe LaPier.)

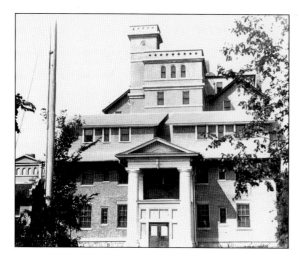

Shown is Gray Gables, the home for teachers at Chazy Central Rural School. Even after that school was in full operation, some youngsters growing up in areas of town now part of the Chazy district continued to attend one-room schoolhouses, some well into the 1940s. (Information, David Martin.)

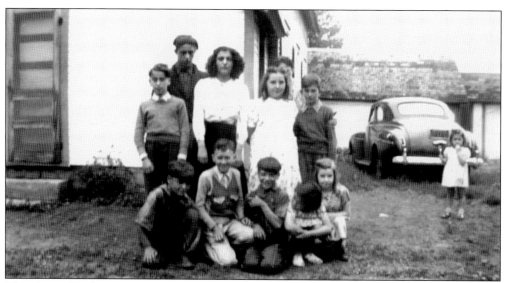

The Hays School, a one-room schoolhouse on the corner of the Ridge Road and Clark Street, is shown c. 1943. From left to right are the following: (front row) Ray Ratta, Gerald Decelle, Virgil Ratta, Theresa Gonyo, and Nancy LaPier; (back row) Donald Hay, Julius Ratta, ? Ratta, Betty LaPier, and Gordon Stiles. The school had eight grades and one teacher. With only one or two students in each grade, everyone got individual attention in each subject. Homework was done while the teacher was instructing other grades. On the walls were a large blackboard and several pull-down maps. The library consisted of one bookcase with books on various subjects. A wood stove provided warmth and a place to dry mittens. The boys and teacher brought in the wood from an outside storage shed. A hand pump provided water for drinking and washing hands. The bathroom was an outhouse, one side for boys and the other for girls. Everyone walked to school. Some came from Route 374, the Hays Road, or the Ashley Road. Some were one and two miles away. Sometimes the teacher, Miss Decelle, would open grapefruit juice or heat up canned pork and beans on a hot plate for lunch. Most of the time, students brought lunch pails to school. Before school was out in the spring, the students and teacher helped clean the school, including the bathrooms. (Information and image, Nancy LaPier LeClair.)

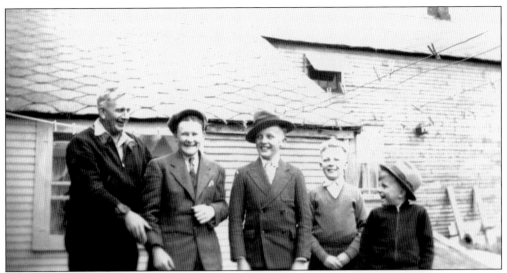

Pictured in this 1940 photograph, from left to right, are Walter Sanger, George Dandrow (the hired man), and Ben, David, and Phillip Sanger. Phillip was born on an Ingraham farm in 1931. The house was heated by a wood stove and had no electricity until 1941. Phillip's mother was "a real queen with a wood stove." Every Friday morning, she made doughnuts and baked fresh bread. Phillip's father was a sugar grower; thus, the family always had maple syrup. The Sangers got their first tractor in 1937. At 14, Phillip joined the Boy Scouts. He once came home from a Boy Scout picnic with a flagpole, which he stored in the barn. When Franklin Delano Roosevelt died in 1945, Phillip was deeply moved. He erected the flagpole in the front yard and ran a flag up to half-mast. This did not go over well with his parents, who were ardent Republicans, but Phillip kept the flag at half-mast for 30 days. (Information, Jessica Lyons and Kelly Bechard; image, Alice Lou Sanger.)

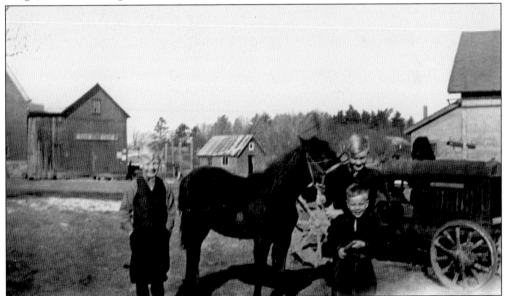

The Sanger boys pose with their tractor. From left to right are David, Ben, and and Phillip (front). The Sangers purchased a McCormick Deering 10-20 in 1937. It was six years old. (Image, Alice Lou Sanger.)

UNITED STATES OF AMERICA
OFFICE OF PRICE ADMINISTRATION

Nº 409532-FE

WAR RATION BOOK No. 3

Void if altered

NOT
VALID
WITHOUT
STAMP

Identification of person to whom issued: PRINT IN FULL

GEORGE   E.   LARAMIE
(First name)   (Middle name)   (Last name)

Street number or rural route   R.F.D. #2

City or post office   Chazy   State   N.Y.

AGE	SEX	WEIGHT	HEIGHT	OCCUPATION
53	M	240 Lbs.	5 Ft. 11 In.	farmer

SIGNATURE   George E. Laramie
(Person to whom book is issued. If such person is unable to sign because of age or incapacity, another may sign in his behalf.)

WARNING

This book is the property of the United States Government. It is unlawful to sell it to any other person, or to use it or permit anyone else to use it, except to obtain rationed goods in accordance with regulations of the Office of Price Administration. Any person who finds a lost War Ration Book must return it to the War Price and Rationing Board which issued it. Persons who violate rationing regulations are subject to $10,000 fine or imprisonment, or both.

OPA Form No. R-130

LOCAL BOARD ACTION

Issued by   2510.1
    (Local board number)   (Date)

Street address _____

City _____ State _____

(Signature of issuing officer)

RATION STAMP NO. 5	RATION STAMP NO. 6	RATION STAMP NO. 7
RATION STAMP NO. 9	RATION STAMP NO. 10	RATION STAMP NO. 11
RATION STAMP NO. 13	RATION STAMP NO. 14	RATION STAMP NO. 15
RATION STAMP NO. 17	RATION STAMP NO. 18	RATION STAMP NO. 19
RATION STAMP NO. 21	RATION STAMP NO. 22	RATION STAMP NO. 23
RATION STAMP NO. 25	RATION STAMP NO. 26	RATION STAMP NO. 27
RATION STAMP NO. 29	RATION STAMP NO. 30	RATION STAMP NO. 31
RATION STAMP NO. 33	RATION STAMP NO. 34	RATION STAMP NO. 35
RATION STAMP NO. 37	RATION STAMP NO. 38	RATION STAMP NO. 39
RATION STAMP NO. 41	RATION STAMP NO. 42	RATION STAMP NO. 43
RATION STAMP NO. 45	RATION STAMP NO. 46	RATION STAMP NO. 47

Shown are a war ration book and some ration stamps. Morris Roberts of Champlain grew up in the 1940s on a West Chazy farm at the corner of the Esker and Slosson Roads. He was one of 13 children, along with Evelyn, Francis, Richard, Pearl, Dora and Doris (twins), Rita and Lita (twins), Ronald, Margaret, Betty, and Gerald. His parents were Wilfred and Elizabeth Ebere Roberts. As the farm had no electricity, the 20 cows had to be milked by the light of lanterns. For amusement, the children would fasten snow fencing from beam to beam in the loft, run across it, and jump into the loose hay. One day, Morris Roberts tried to parachute from the barn roof (some 10 feet from the ground) with an umbrella. The umbrella flipped straight up, and Morris came down fast and hard, spraining his ankle. (Information, Bob Cheeseman.)

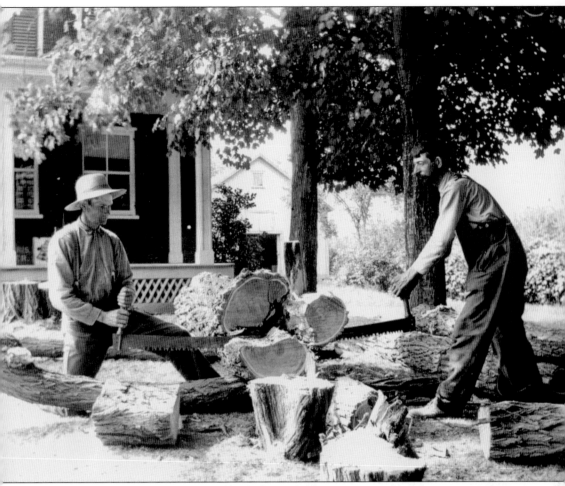

Men are pictured using a crosscut saw. The Roberts children spent much of their time working or playing outdoors. The family cut all of its firewood and used horses to skid the logs out of the woods. The trees were cut down with axes and a two-man crosscut saw. The family had two horses, Molly and Dolly, that must have weighed a ton apiece. They were strong but did not like to work. Three or four carloads of friends and relatives from Canada would come every weekend with food—butter, sugar, and other things that were in short supply during World War II. The family raised chickens for the eggs. One day a week, it was the job of Morris Roberts to deliver the eggs to regular customers in Plattsburgh. Some customers would take a dozen and some two dozen. As pay, Morris's parents would take him to the movies. The hay was handled loose, raked into rows far enough apart to accommodate a wagon, and pitched by hand. The family did not get a tractor until 1946. The children rode the bus to school and always took lunches in dinner pails. One day, on the way home, Morris Roberts and Albert Decelle got into a heated discussion about which automobiles were the best—GM products or Fords. Roberts threw his dinner pail at Decelle and hit him in the back of his head. The bus driver stopped and said, "This will be a lesson to you; you can walk home from here." (Information, Bob Cheeseman; image, David Martin.)

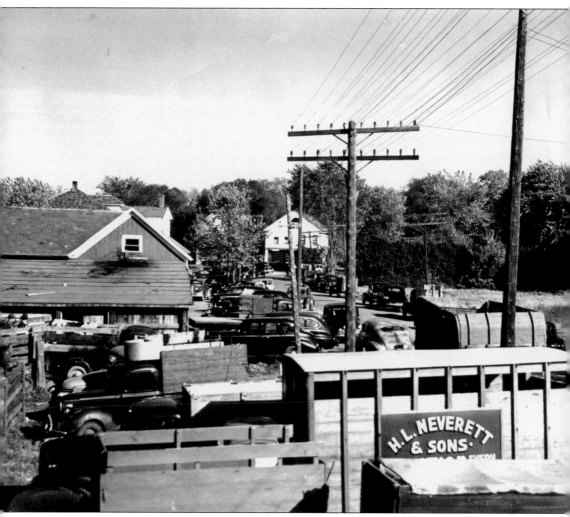

This view looks east along Bank Street during the cattle auction. The Cheeseman family moved to Chazy from King's Bay on May 1, 1944. During World War II, nights meant blackouts, and activities were limited to either listening to the radio or going to bed. Travel out of town was limited by the need for ration stamps for gasoline. A movie at Rouses Point was a big treat. The older children would meet at the railroad station on Saturday and take the 7:00 p.m. train to Rouses Point and return on the 10:00 p.m. train. The stationmaster at the time was a Mr. Dressen. Work trains came along once or twice a week, depending on how much track trouble there was. Another great draw was the weekly cattle sale around the corner at the H.L. Neverett & Sons sale barn. The Neveretts ran the North Farm from the late 1940s through the 1960s. When they had horses to pasture, they would put them near the railroad station east of the river. Jim Blair would come down and lasso horses for Norm Burl, Girard Breyette, and others to ride. (Information, Bob Cheeseman; image, Kim Neverett Howley.)

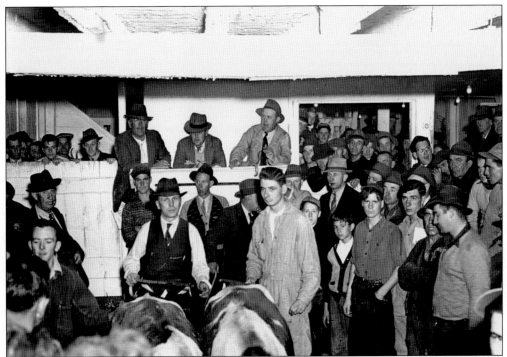

Shown is a cattle sale at the H.L Neverett & Sons barn. Identified from left to right in the foreground are Billy, Harry, and Bob Neverett, Royal Giroux (with his left hand in his pocket), and Stub Spiegel (wearing a hat and a cardigan sweater). (Image, Kim Howley.)

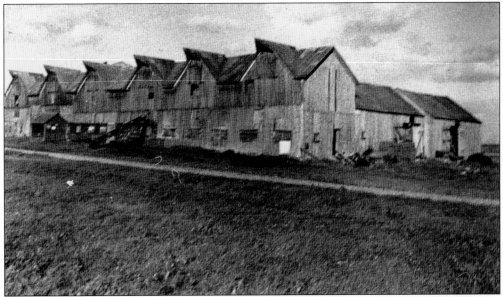

Life was full of hard work on the Gordon Farm, located on the Dunn Road in the town of Chazy. The Ernest Rushford family operated it in the late 1940s and early 1950s. The farm included a large barn with many gables, where the family milked more than 100 cows daily. The family also raised pigs, chickens, and other animals. It was a busy place for the Rushford children, who would even find some excitement chasing down a stray hog.

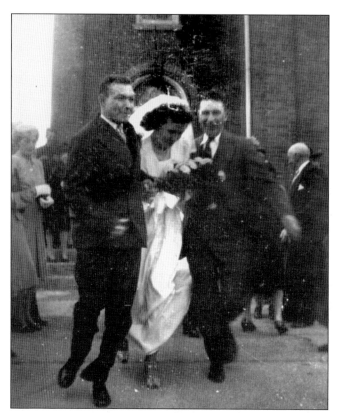

Good friends from their school days, Melvin "Mac" McWhinnie and Esther (Labare) McWhinnie leave the Methodist church in Chazy with Ralph Hislop. The McWhinnies' wedding in 1946 caused big excitement in town, as it had been a long time since young people had been married in Chazy (because of World War II). During the war, McWhinnie served overseas in the army. Friends gave the bride's family their sugar-rationing coupons to be certain there would be a proper wedding cake, and wedding presents included many gas-rationing coupons to help the couple get away for a honeymoon. (Information, Melvin McWhinnie; image, Esther McWhinnie.)

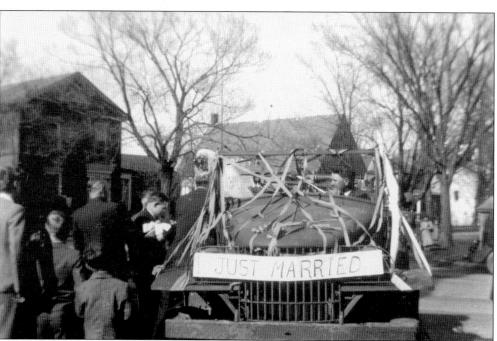

The getaway car for the newlyweds was provided for the couple by the Chazy orchards. The townspeople decorated it. (Image, Esther McWhinnie.)

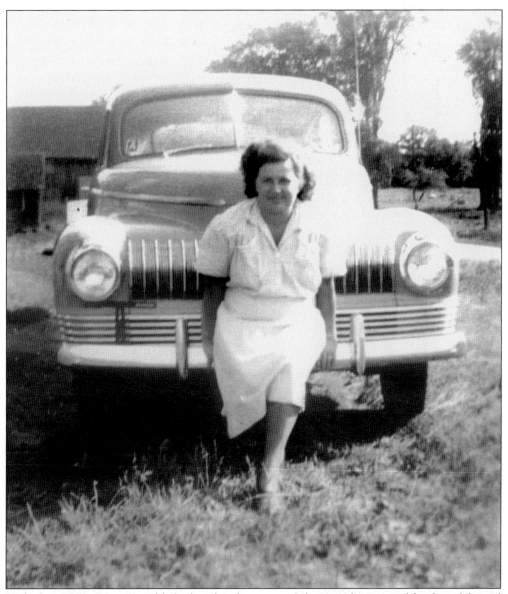

In the late 1930s, Mary Trombly had a job in her native Schenectady as a maid for the celebrated Hollywood actor Charles Coburn, who directed a summer theater festival at Union College. During this time, she met Chazy resident Paul Lewis, who was working for General Electric. At the end of one summer season, the Coburns, thoroughly pleased with Mary's help, asked her to go back to California with them. After some thought, she decided that marrying Lewis and settling in Chazy was more important than going to Hollywood; thus, she declined. Chazy suited her well. An inventive mother of five children—Robert, Richard, Paul, and Gail Lewis—she figured that if they had something to entertain them at home, they would not roam the town. To accomplish her end, she bought a full-sized pool table and put it up in her kitchen. It took up so much room that she had to edge around it to get on with the usual chores of cooking and washing up. However, during the 1950s and 1960s, everyone had fun playing pool, including her. (Information, David Martin; image, Richard Lewis.)

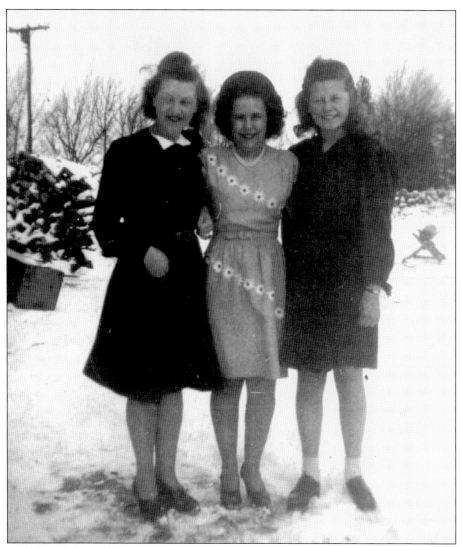

Pictured, from left to right, are Maija Partala, a friend, and Anja Partala in Sciota in 1947. "Bingo tonight at seven o'clock" were the only words of English that Anja Partala knew when she arrived in New York City in March 1947 after a two-week Atlantic crossing from Paris with her mother, Maija Partala. Her mother was going to marry Carroll J. Terrier, a resident of Sciota. She had met him in Paris while working as a single mother in the war-torn city; he was an American serviceman who took part in the liberation of France. She thought she was going to live in New York City, and he did not know enough French to realize that she misunderstood her final destination. The mother and daughter were surprised when they finally arrived at a small house just outside of Sciota with dirt floors and no indoor plumbing. The four months that Anja spent in school in 1947 were spent quietly listening while trying to absorb the language. The family remained in Sciota for about a year and a half and then moved to a small house in West Chazy, where they stayed until Anja graduated from high school in 1952. Terrier then built a home on Route 9 in Chazy across from the Gregware Farm. Anja lived there until she married Robert Earl in 1955. Eventually, she became an American citizen, embracing this country as her own and calling the North Country "home." (Information, Lorna Forster; image, Anja Earl.)

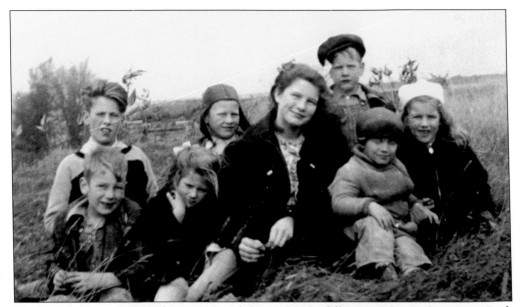

The Earl children of West Chazy are, from left to right, the following: John, Barbara, Jane, Paul, and Dorothy Earl; (back row) Harris, Richard, and Robert Earl. (Image, Tina Trombly.)

Shown is the West Chazy altar boys basketball team of 1945. The team consisted of six boys from West Chazy (two Catholics and four Protestants). Father Laporte was the coach. From left to right are the following: (front row) Ray "Sunny" Mooso, Joe "Pal" LaPier, Lindon Payne, and Jay Payne; (back row) Morris Lucia, Father Laporte, and Richard Earl. (Image, Beverly Payne Christensen.)

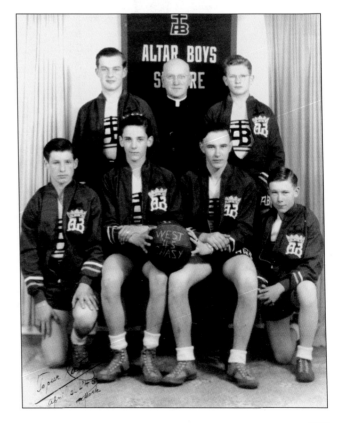

Grandma's Clothesline

I charge through the sheets
Drying on Grandma's clothesline
Pretending to be the bull
That stands in the field
Behind the barn

I make a tee-pee
Out of sheets
And pretend to be the whole Indian
That I am only 1/16th of
Until Grandma says,
"Don't dirty those sheets!"
"But, Gram . . ." I say

I play in Grandma's attic
Dressing up in old clothes
Pretending to be grown up
Gram says, "You'll grow up soon enough."
"But Gram . . ." I say

My cousins and I wait till dark
To play "No Ghosts Are Out Tonight"
We run and laugh until
Gram says, "Come on in before
You catch a cold!"
"But Gram!" we all say

My older cousins say
That there is a BOOGIE MAN
In the cornfield,
Gramma says, "There is no such thing."
But I still get a little bit scared

The only time I ever REALLY got in trouble
with Gram
Was when my cousin Neil and I played
"Who Can Hit The Bottom Cellar Step
With A Tomato"
With Gram's whole bushel full.
My bottom hurt afterwards,
But I sure had fun,
And I think Gramma even laughed,
A little

Now that I'm grown
And don't have to play dress up,
I know my grandmother was right,
Even though I still want to
Charge through the sheets
Like that old bull
Sometimes . . .
—Stephanie Olin
Granddaughter of Ralph and Audrey Dragoon